HAPPY

THE LOST ART OF

TO

CUSTOMER SERVICE

HELP

WRITTEN BY

MICHELE MARSHALL

WITH ANDY EARLE

HAPPY TO HELP

The Lost Art of Customer Service

MICHELE MARSHALL

Dedicated to You

You whom I haven't seen for much too long
This one's for you.
For you know what and
you probably know why.

If there's a book that you want to read, but it hasn't been written yet, then you must write it.

— TONI MORRISON

CONTENTS

INTRODUCTION

"Let me speak to your supervisor."

It was the early 90's and I was working as a customer service agent for a large bank when I received this call from a furious client. She was holding the bank—and by proxy, me—responsible for a recent overdraw on her account. She'd written a postdated check to one of her vendors, who cashed it prematurely, resulting in a substantial overdraw and subsequent overdraft fee on her account.

"You idiots let him cash the check!" she screamed. "It's all your fault!"

I explained that postdated checks are informal agreements between check writers and recipients. Legally, a recipient can cash a check at any time, regardless of the date. I told her the overdraft was her own fault, not ours.

Not a good move.

The client's temper exploded, and she unleashed an irrational tirade on me. My supervisor got on the phone and did his best to calm the woman down. Then he gave her a refund on the overdraft fee for this incident...and the ten other bounced checks on her account. Problem solved, but how did I let this exchange get so out of hand?

First, take a moment to answer this question for yourself: How would you have reacted in this scenario?

If you are reading this book, you can likely relate to my frustration. Whether you're a customer service agent, manager, or business owner, you have dealt with clients desperate to place their mistakes on your shoulders.

The way I reacted to this customer was wrong. There are things I could have done to get the situation back under control, but I didn't do them.

In the decades following this exchange, I've learned through hard-won experience that the "secret sauce" to successful customer service is not about arguing that you are right. Nor is it about proving your point. Or even making the sale.

It's about the customer's experience.

Successful customer service is about showing the customer you care. You do this by turning your reactivity into proactivity and becoming an advocate for your customer. When you work in customer service, you are a powerful lifeline.

I want to encourage you throughout this book to approach your role from a place of empowerment. I'll give you the four pillars to help you have less frustration, more connection, and better business. I have developed these throughout my career specializing in customer service and they work universally in any situation where you're dealing with customers. But before I show you the pillars, we need to talk about what I did wrong on that call about overdrafts. It all comes down to my mindset.

WHY MINDSET MATTERS

In customer service, your mindset is your foundation. Finding your power in customer service starts with being conscious of your internal mental processes. I was making three key mental mistakes in the aforementioned scenario, and I didn't even know it.

MISTAKE #1: I wanted to be right

I was more focused on getting my point across than listening to my customer. I prioritized "rightness" over the customer experience.

Customers come to us because they need our help. As customer service representatives, it's not our job to tell them they are wrong. We're supposed to help them find a solution.

MISTAKE #2: I took the situation personally

I took this customer's unkind words to heart. Although I thought I was speaking in a calm and rational way, I was mad. And my emotions transferred to my vocal tonality. Customers know when we are upset. It's impossible to cover up strong emotions.

MISTAKE #3: I gave away my power

Instead of working with my customer to find a resolution, I handed the problem to my supervisor. Through patience, understanding, respect, and the appropriate know-how, I could have become the "one-stop-shop" for my customer. Instead, I not only made myself feel powerless, I also made my customer feel unimportant; someone who could be handed off.

Now, let's compare this to a later situation where my mindset was in the right place.

Twenty years ago, I started a job in the IT department at a different bank. I knew next to nothing about IT, but I had a decade of experience in customer service. My first major project was overseeing the installation of a new server. On day two, three of the hard drives failed and 30 days of data was completely erased. In order to resolve the issue, our customers needed to re-enter the data manually. This required a significant amount of their time.

After I'd spoken with the customers and informed them of the issue, my boss approached me. "What did you say to these people?" he asked, wide-eyed. "They're upset, but not nearly as mad as I thought they'd be!"

It turns out there are three things I did right to put myself in the right mindset.

SOLUTION #1: I practiced patience and listened to my customers

I took time to genuinely and compassionately listen to our customers and their concerns without internalizing their frustration.

SOLUTION #2: I was transparent in my communication

Although it's important to be discerning in what we tell a customer, honest and transparent communication is critical in building a trusting relationship. Since I was new to IT at the time and didn't have access to the backend of the server, I was not able to identify the issue immediately. However, I told my customers I knew where to find the answers and I reassured them I would address the situation after our call ended. After getting the needed information I called my customers back and guided them step-by-step to resolve the issue.

SOLUTION #3: I cared about helping my customers

I took the initiative to be an advocate on the behalf of my customers. I established communication with our server vendor and worked with them to resolve the issue to the best of their ability. I kept the customer informed during the process so they knew I was working for them. The customers shared with my boss that I was heartbroken on their behalf and had made it my mission to be there for them. They felt I understood their struggle, and that made all the difference.

In the end, we got our customers to work with us and many of them chose to stay with our bank despite the significant IT issue. It goes to show that, regardless of industry, the principle is always the same: **Cultivate the right mindset and you'll get the right result.**

WHY ME?

So, how did I develop the "right" mindset? Here's my story...

Growing up, I abided by this simple principle: If I can help someone, I will.

For much of my childhood, it was just my mom and me. My mom was single, and my siblings were all significantly older than me. They were, for the most part, out of the house by the time I hit puberty.

Being a single parent was hard for my mom, so I found myself taking on the role of "man of the house." This meant I learned how to do everything from changing a tire to fixing a sink.

Here's what else I learned: I love helping people! I also love knowing how to help people. By learning how to help at such a young age I felt like I had a special superpower.

At 14, I joined my mom working at a bank. My job was doing quality checks for credit cards and my desk was right next to the customer service representatives. Every day they would complain to each other, "Wow, this guy's an idiot!" or, "This woman has no clue how to balance her checkbook!" Despite my love of helping people, my first thought was, "Oh, hell no! I never want to work in customer service!"

Which is how I ended up in collections.

If you've never worked in collections, imagine all the stress of customer service, except in this department you have absolutely no hope of a positive interaction with a customer. If in customer service you are an advocate for your customer, in collections you are their executioner.

I hated playing the bad cop. I wanted to get back to being the hero. I wanted to return to my roots and help people...but how could I reconcile that with what I had seen from customer service reps so far?

This question gnawed at me until, one day, I came to the most important revelation of my career: The problem with customer service isn't the institution, but the mindset of the representatives.

I realized stellar customer service requires a representative who works from a positive mental space. To elaborate, let me take you back to an incident that happened when I was learning how to drive.

I was in the backseat of the car while another student drove and the driving instructor sat in the passenger's seat. Suddenly, there was a loud *pop*, and the car began to rumble. The tire had blown out. The other student started crying, the instructor panicked, and I....knew what to do. I calmly changed the tire then comforted the other student and reassured the instructor that it was taken care of.

This real-life situation was, to me, an example of how a person should approach customer service.

Here's the mental space I came from in the above scenario: I owned my ability to take action in a situation,

I prioritized empathy and authenticity, and I embraced the core principle that I adopted as a young child: **If I can help someone, I will.**

Armed with this mental approach, I continued on to a career in customer service at the bank along with other industries like the import/export business, IT, multi-level marketing, and city government. I've been an agent, a supervisor, and even an entrepreneur. I've also run the Manhattan Toastmasters Club and landed it in the distinguished "Perfect 10 Club" four times.

I learned through all of these experiences, both in life and business, that my realization was important. Starting from a good mental space is the bedrock for an all around positive customer service experience.

Takeaway: A career in customer service grows out of how good you can make the customer feel. A good experience starts with a good mindset.

WHY NOW?

This is not the first book on customer service, nor will it be the last, but in a rapidly evolving world we all need to be consistently reminded to make others feel seen and heard. Good customer service comes down to making people feel like they matter.

One of my current positions is managing the IT support team for the government of a large city. There is a reason why going to the DMV has become synonymous with dehumanization. I look around at the customer service representatives in government and I see a shocking amount of apathy. Many employees will not even make direct eye contact with their customers.

When dealing with a customer in person, it is near impossible to make them feel like anything other than 'just a number' when you won't look them in the eye.

In the past 15 years, I've witnessed the disintegration of common decency and kindness in the service industry. The "DMV experience" seems more of the norm than the exception in customer service, even outside of government. I see a world where individualism is replacing the crucial sense of caring.

Kindness should not have to be taught, but it does.

Following 2020, we are at the beginning of a worldwide revolution in the way we conduct business. Although we are seeing exponential growth through e-commerce, digital expansionism, and AI integration, these cannot replace or circumvent the importance of a connection with another human being. It is essential that we reevaluate the way we lay our foundation for customer service because it will set the precedent for generations to come. Twenty years from now, will we be connected or will we be disconnected?

Workers coming into customer service right now don't know what they don't know. Generation Z employees who have been raised around depleted customer service experiences might not be aware of the powerful roles that respect, empathy, knowledge, and kindness play in developing a business. I want to help instill these principles, so we know that the future of business lies in the hands of people who possess a genuine desire and ability to help.

This book is not just for customer service representatives, either. **Customer service is relevant at *every single level*: as a service representative, as a supervisor, as a business owner, and as a human being.** Every position can be treated as a customer service position because every day you are interacting with people and having an impact on their life experience. Treating someone like they matter is always worth it. Yesterday, today, and tomorrow.

BECOMING AN ADVOCATE

In customer service, you are in the business of creating a customer journey that is fulfilling. You are not a taskmaster, or disciplinarian, or middleman. Your most important role is as an **advocate** for your customer.

Being an advocate means you are personally responsible for ensuring your customer receives the help they need.

As an advocate, you embody three primary archetypes:

ARCHETYPE #1: The Savior

You are a lifeline. Imagine someone calls into your line in a complete panic. It is your job to "just take care of it." Your customer doesn't need a long-winded explanation of what went wrong. She just needs you to fix it.

ARCHETYPE #2: The Teacher

Sometimes a customer comes to you because they are experiencing a recurring issue or they are new to a product and need to learn how it works. It is your job in this role to "walk them through it." Most people prefer to be walked through the process rather than read all the manuals. It is up to you to take on the role of teacher and guide them toward an ongoing positive experience with your product or services.

ARCHETYPE #3: The Sounding Board

Sometimes the most difficult role is listening. Often in customer service, we are simply there to be the icon of causality. It is your job in these moments to listen to your customer's complaints without judgement. Dealing with these frustrated customers can be disheartening. They can even make you feel disempowered. To help you subvert these feelings, keep this in mind: As a listener who is an advocate, you do not need to be a martyr. You only need to embody the empathy and wisdom to know when someone just needs to talk it out for themselves. By allowing that space, you are advocating for your customer by granting them the right to be heard.

Approaching each of these archetypes with the mindset of an advocate allows you to work toward a concrete result for your customer. In my experience, you can tell which archetype your customer needs you to be within the first minute of a call.

YOU ARE A "YOU," NOT A "WE"

Being an advocate means you take personal responsibility for your customer.

As a customer service agent, you are not a "we," and your customer is not a "they". You have a name. Your customer has a name. You are each individuals.

In other words, when you answer the phone and say, "We are here to help our customers," you are devaluing yourself and your customer. You both feel like one among many.

No one wants a script. They want a connection. So instead of, "We are here to help you," change the narrative to, "I am here to help you."

The benefits of this are two-fold: 1) You will feel empowered to take personal ownership as the single point of contact in helping your customer, and 2) You will empower your customer to feel like they are more than just a number. They are a human being whose thoughts, experiences, and name matter...and they have you in their corner.

How do you establish this connection? Here are a few tips to get you started:

1. Refer to yourself as an "I" and your customer as a "You."
2. Learn your customer's name and use your name as well. (Hint: If you don't want to give them your name for personal reasons, you can use an alias....but own that alias as you would your own name.)
3. If you are dealing with someone in person, look them in the eye.
4. Make sure your body language is welcoming, confident, and reassuring. This means you don't

cross your arms or turn your body away from your customer unnecessarily.

5. Be wary of your tone. Vocal tone indicates intent. If your intent is anything other than, "I want to help you," that will reflect in your voice. Clarify and remind yourself of intent before any interaction with a customer.

YOU ARE A LEADER

To be an effective advocate, you must also be a leader. You have to lead a customer from where they are to where you want them to go. That starts with meeting a customer where they are at.

Many customer service agents believe they are last in line when solving a problem. As a result, they set high expectations for what a customer *should* already know. The customer *should* have consulted your online troubleshooter. And read the full product documentation. And watched the tutorial video on setting up the product properly.

Here's the reality: You are typically the first call.

You cannot approach a customer with a preconceived notion of what they *should* know. "You signed up for this credit card, how do you not know how it works?" Many people are not that detail-oriented. When was the last time you read the entire manual for your new phone, refrigerator, or table?

Let's go back to my first example of the woman with the postdated check. I would have handled that scenario better if I had reduced my expectations of what my customer already knew. As an employee of the bank, I knew that anyone could legally cash a postdated check before the date listed. Did my customer know that? Obviously not. By accepting that she lacked knowledge, I could have cultivated the patience necessary to guide her to a resolution.

Your customers most likely haven't read all the terms and conditions for your business. Just because they've bought a product does not mean they are intimately, or even passingly, familiar with it. Imagine you are an ambassador for a foreign country. Your customers often don't know the country's language or customs, and it is up to you to show them the landscape from the moment they step off the plane.

Tourists *love* to ask questions. "What is that?" "Why did that happen?" "Why can't we go there?" You play a vital role in leading a customer through their journey, one step at a time. That means you sometimes have to answer these questions to help them take the steps themselves, and sometimes it means you just pick them up and put them on the next step.

Remember: You are the leader. It is up to you, not your customer, to determine how best to proceed.

Once I had an irate client who called because her email was malfunctioning. My company was a subsidiary company owned by the business that controlled the email software, so I didn't have access to the backend. When I relayed this information to my customer, she started going down the dreaded *"Why"* rabbit trail. "*Why* did this happen? *Why* do you have to contact this other company? *Why* does the email shut off when I try to print? *Why* does my email not update my appointments?" While I was transparent in my answers, I refrained from being overly descriptive in my responses.

Why? Because curiosity is not the same as interest. Answering these questions at length would not resolve the issue at hand or subvert my customer's frustrations. It would simply waste time. In this scenario, I told the customer I needed to resolve the issue on the backend and asked whether she wanted me to address the questions in detail or "just taking care of it." Her response? "You know what? You're right. I don't want to know." The problem was resolved quickly without the 30-minute penalty of the "Why" rabbit trail.

At the end of the day, you want your customer to feel like they either don't have to call back or they can always call back. Either way, you have to reliably lead them to a resolution.

A company that is adept at this is GoDaddy. They set a standard operating procedure for their representative to always give their customer the option. They can walk you through it or they can just fix it for you. Give your customer the choice. Do they need a savior, an instructor, or a sounding board?

Giving your customer an option means you are being a proactive leader.

You can only do this when you equip yourself with the knowledge necessary to address your customer in the way they need to be addressed. Does the customer need you to be a savior? Learn how to resolve problems quickly. Is the customer looking for a teacher? Don't only learn how to fix an issue, but learn how to teach someone else how to fix it. What about a customer who just needs to scream it out for 10 minutes? Learn how to arm yourself with patience, empathy, perceptiveness, strength...and maybe a small piece of chocolate to reward yourself for being a good human being.

THE FOUR PILLARS OF GREAT CUSTOMER SERVICE

My hope is that you now appreciate the importance of mindset in customer service and the immediate threats we face to the future of the customer service industry. I also expect you've learned a few ways to reevaluate your role so you can help customers in the way they need to be helped.

The rest of this book will equip you to provide great customer service throughout your career. You're going to learn my four pillar system for customer service success. Together, I call these four pillars "The **P.U.R.E. System.**" This stands for:

Patience

Understanding

Respect

Experience

Why the word "pure"? According to my favorite standard, the Merriam Webster dictionary, "pure" has three definitions that I believe are perfectly aligned with good customer service:

pure \ *pyür*

¹ : free from harshness or roughness and
   being in tune
² : free from what vitiates, weakens, or
   pollutes
³ : having exactly the talents or skills
   needed for a particular role

Keeping these definitions in mind, ask yourself three important questions as your read through this book:

- *How can I be more in tune with my customer?*
- *How can I rid myself of habits that weaken relationships with customers?*
- *How can I ensure that I am equipped to give the best service to my customer?*

Through the P.U.R.E. system, you'll use the qualities of patience, understanding, and respect to create fulfilling and rewarding customer service experiences for your customers. You'll walk away knowing how to empower yourself, your customer, and your business. So with our sights set high, let's dive into Pillar One: Patience.

PILLAR ONE:

PATIENCE

PILLAR ONE: PATIENCE

The key to extraordinary customer service

As Geoffrey Chaucer once said, *"Patience is a conquering virtue."* This is all too true, especially when it comes to customer service.

With due respect to Mr. Chaucer, since my aim is to help cultivate quality customer service in the modern era and beyond, I'm going to employ a more contemporary analogy for patience.

Patience is like The Force.

Yes, I do mean The Force from Star Wars. If you're not a Star Wars junkie, bear with me, there are relatable nuggets in here for you too...but who doesn't love a little extra Baby Yoda in their day?

According to the official Star Wars website[1], The Force is defined as,

*"A mysterious energy field created by life that binds the galaxy together. Harnessing the power of **The Force** gives the Jedi, the Sith, and others sensitive to this spiritual energy extraordinary abilities, such as levitating objects, tricking minds, and seeing things before they happen."*

In psychological literature, patience is defined as,

"The propensity of a person to wait calmly in the face of frustration, adversity, or suffering[2]."

No, patience will not give you the ability to levitate boulders or suck out someone's lifeforce, but it is the mysterious energy that holds the world of customer service together. And it *does* give you the power to be sensitive to and control any interaction, "mind-meld" with your customer, and predict how a situation will play out.

Patience is The Force behind good customer service.

Using this analogy, think of yourself like a Customer Service Jedi. You must learn to control your patience because it will serve as the foundation for every other pillar. Need to foster understanding? Start with patience. Want to show respect? You get there through patience. Trying to create a results-driven experience for your customers? You can lead your customers to the best results by *patiently* working with them.

Through patience, you can empower yourself and your customer to find a solution and build positive, long-lasting rapport.

Succumb to the "dark side" (aka impatience) and you run

the risk of sidestepping a solution, destroying your customer's trust in you, and damaging their confidence in your company.

Patience is the key. This is the way.

MATTER PATIENCE DOES

"You will find only what you bring in."

— *YODA*

Patience is the soil from which every other quality you need in customer service grows: empathy, warmth, trust, and care. When you equip yourself with patience, you encourage these other valuable qualities to flourish. These character attributes will help you have a successful and rewarding conversation with your customer.

From your customer's point of view, your patience will make them feel heard, respected, and cared for. With the simple quality of patience, you can assure your customer they are not just another number in your system, but are valued by both you as their representative and by your company as a whole.

Treat your customer like royalty and you will gain their loyalty.

Also, patience is a *reciprocal* quality. When you *bring* in patience, you will find patience waiting for you. Ipso facto when you give patience to your customer, they will give you patience in return. Through your display of patience, your customer will understand that you are with them. If you are with them, 99% of the time they will be with you.

At this point, you might think, "But wait, *the customer* is calling *me*, a customer service representative. Shouldn't they already *know* I'm on their side?"

In today's world of customer service this is far from a given. Many customers are jaded from their prior negative encounters with impatient representatives. They may approach the conversation expecting they will need to fight to be heard. Patience quickly disarms the battle-ready customer. In the long term, this reciprocal relationship will allow you to build comfortable trust with your customer.

Conversely, when you enter the conversation with impatience, you will find impatience on the other end. *You* will be the one laying the grounds for battle because you've already made your customer feel like they will need to fight to get their point across.

Remember: You are in control of the conversation. It is your obligation to set the correct tone from the start with patience.

What are the consequences of impatience?

The mildest consequence you will see is customer dissatisfaction. You are a representative of your company. Whatever your customer feels about you will be projected onto your company as a whole. When your customer feels undervalued and unheard due to your impatient attitude, they will feel like the company does not care about them or their business. If they can, the customer will then seek out competitors who make them feel valued.

If your company has a monopoly in your industry or your customer is locked into a long-term contract, that doesn't mean you're out of the woods. While the customer may be unable to extricate themselves from your services, there is a good chance they will retaliate via negative feedback. While this may simply extend to complaining to a few close friends, if the interaction is bad enough, it could lead to negative online reviews.

A few statistics gathered to demonstrate the impact of negative reviews[3]:

1. Only 13% of consumers even consider buying from companies with a 1 or 2 star rating (out of 5 stars)
2. For the average consumer, 3.3 stars is the minimum rating they need to use a company's products or services
3. 94% of consumers say that a negative review convinced them to avoid a company
4. With just one negative blog or article, 22% of all business can be lost. With three negative articles, this number jumps to 59.2%

Customer retaliation is no joke.

You wield tremendous power in any customer service situation. One dissatisfied customer can break your business, particularly if you are a small business serving a small region. Arming yourself with patience will help protect you and your business from suffering these consequences. While you can't prevent negative reviews altogether, you can significantly reduce their likelihood.

A PATIENT DEMEANOR

"Control, control, you must learn control!"

— *YODA*

At times, patience requires an extraordinary amount of self-control. In my experience, the easiest way to get our minds acclimated to patience is to start by controlling our physical manifestations of impatience. In other words, we must actively cultivate a patient demeanor.

Demeanor is a person's appearance and behavior. It is essentially how other people perceive us. A patient demeanor conveys a sense of warmth, caring, and authenticity. With a patient demeanor, your client will feel you are genuinely on their side. They will sense they can trust your words and actions. Conversely, with an impatient demeanor, you will convey a sense of apathy and alienation. No customer wants to feel like you are counting down the minutes to the next call. This type of demeanor will ultimately cause your customer to lose trust in you as their advocate.

Be aware of what signals an impatient demeanor. I've compiled a list of the most common behaviors in customer service that signal an impatient demeanor.

While many of these symptoms of impatience might be familiar to you, it's essential to be sure you are aware of them. When you are aware of a behavior, you have the power to change it. Further, when you consciously change your actions to present a more patient demeanor, it will influence your mental state. When you act more patient, you feel more patient, because you are more patient.

As you read through this list, take a moment to consider whether you are guilty of these behaviors (most of us are). Awareness is the first step toward change.

Common impatient behavior:

- Lack of eye contact
- Eyes darting to events around you or, worse yet, to the clock
- Drumming Fingers
- Fidgeting
- Audible sighs
- Tongue clicking
- Quick, curt responses (e.g. "Yes. No. I don't know.")
- Condescending tone (e.g. "Ma'am, have you actually tried unplugging it and plugging it back in?")
- Interrupting the customer (e.g. "Sir. Sir. Sir. Will you JUST LISTEN TO ME?")
- Reading directly from the service manual
- Excess use of filler noises like "Mmmhmm" or "Uh-huh"
- Use of industry jargon without explanation
- Using "Sir" or "Ma'am"

Many of us are familiar in our day-to-day interactions with the visual indications of impatience, so I believe I can safely say these actions don't need further elaboration. However, since so many customer service interactions take place over the phone, I'd like to spend a moment elaborating on the verbal indications of impatience.

While many representatives know that curt responses, a condescending tone, or interrupting your customers are classic no-nos, you might be surprised to hear that reading straight from your manager-approved service manual can signal impatience. While the service manual is a useful tool to guide interactions, scripted word-for-word responses can come across as unnatural and robotic. It leaves your customer with the impression that instead of actively listening and responding to their individual query, you are anxiously rushing them through the industry-ok'd motions. *The customer responded in this way? Refer to section 8b.* The customer can hear the canned response in your voice and will leave the conversation faring no better than if they had called an automatic response line.

The solution to sidestepping the 'canned response' effect isn't to throw out your manual. Study your manual and modify it in accordance with how you talk to other humans. Use your own lingo and build your knowledge about your business to the point where you are confident you can formulate a response without consulting the manual. Then you can be fully present and attentive to your customer instead of frantically flipping through *the book* to find the answer.

People call in because they want an actual human being to talk to. This is one more reason why AI can never fully take over human-to-human interaction. How many times have you yelled into the phone: "REPRESENTATIVE!"? Being patient means being present enough to genuinely listen without succumbing to the urge to anxiously grasp at a solution.

Now, let's talk a little bit about the "Mmhmms" and the "Uh-huhs."

In person, if you are speaking with someone, making eye contact, and using these verbal fillers, it can *sometimes* translate to engagement or interest. This is why many of us don't think twice about using them when we are speaking on the phone. However, the hamster wheel of "Mmmhmms" and "Uh-huhs" over the phone can be perceived less as engagement and more as trying to move your customer along through their issue while simultaneously playing Candy Crush under your desk.

Think of the verbal fillers in this context: These are the same noises you might make when talking to your 96-year-old grandma over the phone as she tells you for the 47th time that she suspects the communists have been stealing her green jello. "Mmmhmm. Yeah. Uh-huh. Totally." Resistance may be futile with grandma, but you are not hired to resolve her jello situation. Your customer, on the other hand, needs reassurance that you are actively listening.

Consider this: Customers will often ramble and repeat information when they hear verbal fillers because they are not confident that you are listening. Therefore, the irony of using "Mmhmms" and "Uh-huhs" to move the conversation along is that *because* the customer is more prone to repeat themselves, the call will take longer.

Instead of using filler phrases, summarize and repeat back the customer's issue. "What I hear you saying is that you are having trouble printing your document." This way, you will reassure your customer that you have heard them and you can both feel comfortable moving on toward a solution.

Now, onto jargon. It is deceptively easy, after years working in a business, to think that common terms you use in your industry every day should also be known to your customer. Often, I'll hear impatient customer service agents using jargon to get to the solution more rapidly. "Oh, we simply have to reprogram the CPU microcode!" Meanwhile, the customer is left asking, "What does that mean? What does that mean? What does THAT mean?" The result is that your customer feels inept and you actually extend the conversation by having to double back to clarify your statements. This will lead to frustration for *both of you.*

Make no mistake, it is far easier to use jargon than to explain a complex concept. Part of patience, however, is simplifying your language so you can meet your customer where they're at. To do this, spend a little time translating your industry jargon into everyman language that even your 96-year-old grandmother would understand. Remember that your customer is likely a foreigner to your industry, so your language must be as accessible to them as it was to you when you started out in your business.

Lastly, let's discuss using "Sir" or "Ma'am." As customer service agents, we are taught to prioritize politeness. However, in the modern era where social familiarity in business is more common, personalization can supersede the importance of politeness. This is particularly true when you are trying to form long-lasting rapport with your customer.

As I noted in the previous chapter: You have a name and your customer has a name. Using formal alternatives to a name indicates that you don't have the patience to take the 2 seconds to learn your customer's name. When you learn their name and use it, they feel you've taken the time to see them as an individual and not just another "Sir." It will instill confidence in your customer that you, specifically, are there to guide him, specifically, to a solution.

There is no better way to get someone's attention than by using their name. If you've watched the Mandalorian, you'll remember the scene where we learn the true name of "Baby Yoda." "Baby Yoda" was sitting with Mando and Ahsoka and looking around, seemingly uninterested, until Mando said his name (*spoiler alert*): "Grogu." What happened? He quickly looked at Mando like, "Who, me?" There is power in a name. When you learn your customer's name and use it, you create an instant link between you and your customer.

Now that we've covered some common cues of impatience. Let's do a quick review of some patient demeanor attributes.

Ideal attributes of a patient demeanor:

- Eye contact
- Nodding your head
- Not fidgeting
- Leaning forward
- Responding in an authentic, natural way
- Repeating the customer's query to reassure them
- Taking the time to simplify and clarify complex concepts
- Using your customer's name

A patient demeanor can be exhausting to maintain, particularly with frustrating customers. Thankfully it is like a muscle. The more you use it, the stronger it will become. The beautiful thing about actively cultivating a patient demeanor is that even if you begin the conversation in an impatient frame of mind, your calmness will naturally signal to your brain that you feel patient. Over time and with practice, the patient demeanor will not only relax your customer, but you as well.

THE NEXT STEP: TRAINING TO BE A "CUSTOMER SERVICE JEDI"

"You must feel the Force around you. Here. Between you, me, the tree, the rock, everywhere, yes. Even between the land and the ship."

— *YODA*

Once you are conscious of your demeanor, it's time to take your patience training to the next level. This means actively working to harness patience in all you do. To do this, you need to build a "patience toolkit" in which you carry qualities that go hand-in-hand with patience: listening, trustworthiness, knowledge, curiosity, and leadership.

Here are five rules for building your patience toolkit:

RULE #1: LISTEN YOU MUST

The golden rule of patience is that you first need to listen, then you can respond.

Sounds simple, right?

However, listening, in this case, means *active listening*. It means you are not only hearing the words but are using patience to process what is being said before prematurely developing an opinion. As customer service agents — especially those who are experienced — it can be easy to develop an aura of jadedness where we believe we immediately know the answer because we've seen it all before. This can lead us down a dark path of hastily-made conclusions. As we'll explore later in this chapter, customers rarely present their real issue upfront. It is important, therefore, that we take the time to listen and uncover what the problem truly is before taking action toward a solution.

Even if you do know the correct answer, consider that sometimes a customer needs to tell their full story in order to feel heard and valued. They want a sense of resolution to their tale. Listening will allow them that grace.

I'll add this: **When you are truly listening, you will hear not only what is being said but what is not being said.**

Active listening will help you hear what is behind the rambling, or the rabbit hole questions, or even the yelling. It will allow you to hear intent. Remember the archetypes. Who does your customer need you to be on this call? Do they need a teacher? A sounding board? A savior? The only way you can assess which role you need to fill is by listening.

When I was working at a Bank call center, an irate customer called in because the ATM had "eaten" his ATM card. Unfortunately, in order to get a new one, he had to wait a few hours while the card was processed and then go to the nearest branch to retrieve it.

The customer was ready for a fight.

I provided him with the bottom-line information and then...I listened. He was not happy that he had to wait, and he let me know in no uncertain terms what he was feeling. But still, I stayed on the line and listened. Why? Because what the customer needed in that moment was for his frustration to be heard. Sometimes, all your customer needs is someone to be there with them during a challenging situation and say, "I know, this really sucks." This man didn't need any further information. What he needed was compassion. How did I know what he needed? I listened.

At the end of the call, he had calmed down and I was able to provide his new ATM card with minimal hassle.

RULE #2: BUILD TRUST YOU MUST

Trust is established over time. In the course of one call, you don't have much time with your customer, but patience allows you to lay the groundwork for trust. And believe me, trust matters. Without trust, your search for a solution will feel more like a battle than a collaborative effort toward resolution.

How do you lay the tracks for trust? Follow these steps:

1. Learn and use your customer's name. Remember the "Baby Yoda" example.
2. Give them your name so they know who you are. If you are uncomfortable giving your real name, you can use a pseudonym (be sure to let your coworkers in on your chosen pseudonym!)
3. Get their contact information early, particularly if you are on the phone. Many companies are not set up to return dropped calls to the original representative. Getting transferred from agent to agent sullies the trust your customer has in your business, even if it's the fault of the phone company. You do not want a call to be dropped after 30 minutes of working toward a solution together only to make your customer start from Square One with a new agent. Just imagine your customer on the other end of that dropped call screaming "Noooooo!" a la Darth Vader. It's not a happy thought. Getting your customer's information ensures they have a direct lifeline to you even if the call is dropped. Then, they can rest assured that you are determined to see their problem resolved even if you are disconnected.

4. If you are sending them an email with follow-up information, send it while you are on the phone with the customer. As a Michele with one 'l' and a Marshall with two 'l's', I cannot tell you just how many times my email has been misspelled and I have missed out on an important message. If your customer is like me, they have acute anxiety about losing an email just because of a tricky name. Take the time to send the email with your customer still on the phone. They'll breathe easy when they see in real time that you have followed through.

5. Give your customer the full picture. Tell them exactly what happens when they do follow your instructions and also what will happen if they do not follow through. Armed with your upfront approach, they know they can rely on you to give them the BS-free answer. That trust means they'll also be more likely to follow through than not.

RULE #3: GIVE KNOWLEDGE YOU MUST

Ideally, as a customer service agent, you should know what you're talking about so you don't come off as a robot reciting sermons straight from your customer service manual. You also need to be a direct resource for your customer without referring them to additional materials. No customer wants to be given homework by customer service.

A friend of mine recently needed help setting up a webinar. She thought she needed a business account with the video conferencing company in order to accommodate the large number of attendees (she didn't). In order to help her out, I called customer service on her behalf. Within the first few minutes, the rep told us to read an article. Suddenly my friend, who overheard the comment from the other room, exclaimed, "But I already read the d*** article!" I stayed on the phone with the agent a little longer, and came to realize he in fact knew exactly how to help us. No article needed.

When a customer calls, they want to talk to you. They don't want to read an article or watch a tutorial video. There is no reason why you should ever direct a customer to an outside resource for an explanation when you have the answer at your fingertips. A customer should not be assigned the headache of homework on top of their existing frustrations. In all likelihood, they have done their own research and they still don't understand how to solve their problem. They need *your* help.

When you instruct your customer to read the information on their own, they may leave the conversation thinking, *"Why did I even waste my time calling?"* Take the time to share the full extent of your knowledge and your customer will find value in your services.

RULE #4: ASK QUESTIONS YOU MUST

Here's a shocking statistic from my experience: 70% of people who call in will not directly state their actual issue. It's human nature. Imagine you're in a room with a colleague and you are *freezing*. Most people—especially if they don't know the other person well—will not say "I'm cold." Most of the time they'll ask questions like "Is it cold in here? Do you need a sweater?"

As a customer service representative, you'll often need to read between the lines to uncover the real issue. Be curious. Ask your own questions.

Sometimes, patience means asking a question instead of making a statement.

Take, for example, the situation with the customer service rep helping with my friend's online video meeting. If, instead of saying, "Read this article for the answer," he had asked, "Have you read this article?" he would have quickly learned the article did not contain the answer to my friend's question. As a bonus, he would have avoided incurring my friend's wrath.

The majority of the time, the real question is buried under several qualifying questions. It's like peeling back the layers of an onion to get to the heart of the problem. You can begin with asking a question such as, "What would you like to accomplish in this call?" and then refine the direction from there with follow-up questions. By asking questions from the outset, you can more quickly clarify your customer's intent.

Be wary of how you stage these questions. "What would you like to accomplish in this call?" is very different from, "Why did you call?", which will produce a very different answer.

RULE #5: YOUR ALLY YOUR CUSTOMER IS

Once you get to the true root of the issue, it's time to find a solution. Within customer service, you often must enlist your customer to help in resolving an issue. And, guiding a customer to a solution step-by-step can sometimes require an extraordinary amount of patience, particularly if they do not know your industry well.

When I worked in one IT department in the early 2000's, I had a customer call in with an application error on her desktop. In order to resolve the issue, the customer needed to reinstall the app. At the time, it wasn't feasible to make the repair remotely, so I had to enlist my caller to help in the repair. The customer, who was self-admittedly not tech-savvy, was nervous about this. I could practically hear the panic attack behind every click on her keyboard.

Determined to have a positive interaction, I did four important things: First, I took a deep breath to calm myself so I could help calm my customer (hey, us reps need to breathe sometimes too!). Second, I reasserted that her help was necessary to repair the corrupted application. Third, I reassured her that I was knowledgeable and I would guide her through step-by-step. Fourth, I used simple, jargon-free language so she could follow my instructions without feeling like she was trying to learn rocket science.

The result? This easy-to-follow, clear, concise, and patient advice made it simple for both of us to travel from point A to point B. At the end of the 20-minute conversation, my caller had gone from full on meltdown to tears of gratitude.

RESISTING THE "DARK SIDE"

"When you look at the dark side careful you must be, for the dark side looks back."

— *YODA*

You've mastered the patient demeanor. You've added some new tools to your patience toolbox. But just when you start to feel like Luke Skywalker incarnate...you get that one customer.

The one who calls your line at 4:59 PM on a Friday and decides they need to tie you up for a 30 minute torture session of rabbit hole questioning. It just so happens you have a hot date scheduled at 5:30 PM and your commute is precisely 28 minutes. Your cool, calm exterior is beginning to crack. You feel yourself giving in to the dark side and, within a matter of 20 seconds, all the hard work you've done to become a Jedi of customer service goes down the drain as you sit in your chair drumming your fingers, mmhmm-ing, and offering up quick fixes to try and get your customer the heck off the phone.

Where did it all go wrong?

First things first: forgive yourself. It's ok. We all make mistakes. Maintaining patience in customer service is challenging. It's hard to resist the dark side of impatience when we feel work impinging on our non-work lives.

Have you ever called a customer service line at 4:59 thinking you just made the deadline only to be greeted by an endless ringing? That is a customer service agent who has decided not to pick up. Customer service agents are by no means perfect and that's ok.

While lapses are to be expected, if you give into the dark side too often, it will become increasingly tempting to fall back on impatience. Only one demeanor can be habitual for you. Make it patience.

Arm yourself with a few tools to keep you from reaching your boiling point. These measures will safeguard both you and your customer from any potential explosions of impatience.

Here are a few tips to help you resist the dark side:

TIP #1: MAY THE PAUSE BE WITH YOU

One of the biggest challenges a customer service agent can face is a customer who is talking a mile a minute. When you can't get a word in edgewise, it is difficult to give someone a solution.

When I was working at a call center coaching customer service reps, I had to break my frustrated representatives from their habit of interrupting rambling customers with questions such as "Are you done now?" or "Are you ready for me to help you?" These responses are akin to throwing a stick of dynamite into the middle of a conversation, but I could tell my agents were at their wit's end and thought this was the *only way* to get their customer's attention.

It is not the only way. In fact, there is no quicker way to escalate a situation—and in some cases extend the call—than to condescendingly interject in the middle of a customer's sentence. Alternatively, remember that at some point your customer will need to breathe. Train yourself to look for that half-second pause and take advantage of it.

Consider this *patient* approach to rambling customers:

1. First, find that half-second pause.
2. Get their attention with their name. "Grogu, may I call you Grogu?" This will automatically make them zero in on what you are saying.
3. Repeat back to them what you have identified as their primary issue. "Grogu, I hear you're having difficulty locating your shipment of giant frog eggs." Customers often ramble because they are worried their point is not getting across. Repeating to them what you understand the issue to be will reassure them you have paid attention and are ready to move with them toward the next stage of resolution.
4. Now that they feel assured you've heard their issue, they are ready to work with you toward a solution. "Grogu, our records indicate your shipment was signed for by a Mr. Mandalorian on April 22. If you haven't already, will you check with Mr. Mandalorian to see if he has your shipment?"

This patient, yet firm, approach will help the customer feel confident in both you and the resolution.

TIP #2: A JEDI YOUR CUSTOMER IS NOT

Your customer doesn't know what they don't know. Part of patience comes from embracing the reality that your customer is not, in fact, an idiot...they just simply do not know what you know. It is up to you to be their guide.

So, instead of getting frustrated because you think your customer is a complete ignoramus, convert the narrative to something like this: "In this situation, I am the Jedi Master and it is my duty to use this power to help this person." Remember, your caller isn't the Jedi.

You are the Jedi. And "with great power comes great responsibility."

This acknowledgement of the role you hold and the power you wield will help you to cultivate empathy. Empathy will lead to patience. If you struggle to have empathy for your customer, remember this: At some point, on some other call, someone else will need to be your Jedi Master. How would you want them to help guide you?

TIP #3: CODDLE DO NOT

While it is important to cultivate empathy, there is a point of coddling. If you give into appeasing your customer too much, you'll lose your power over the situation. Over time this can lead to a lot of pent-up rage that will, undoubtedly, explode at some point.

Customers that elicit the "coddling" response generally fall into three categories:

1. Customers who are inattentive
2. Customers who are combative
3. Customers who are codependent

With each of these customer categories, there is one surefire way to avoid coddling: Leadership. Time to pull out that "leadership" quality from your patience toolkit. You are in control of the flight plan so it is up to you to keep the ship moving forward. Coddling will only keep you and your customers stuck.

Leadership applies to each of these categories of customers. With customers who are inattentive, it is important to guide them toward a reasonable timeline.

Recently, a frustrated client of mine called in because he was locked out of his online account. It turned out his account kept getting locked because he was still logged onto another computer. As I was trying to assist the customer, he was engaging in side conversations, making it challenging to get him to listen to me long enough to hear the resolution. In the end, I had to repeat myself about 8 times before he actually heard my instruction. My brother overheard this conversation and said, "I don't understand how you have the patience to deal with these people!"

How *did* I find the patience to deal with this customer? I told him my plan to fix the issue and then asked him to call me back when he had taken the action steps necessary and could move on to the next stage of resolution. This way, I allowed the customer to set a timeline that worked for him and call back when he could be present.

Customers get combative because they feel powerless in a situation. The solution is not to coddle them by saying, "Sir, please calm down," or apologizing profusely in the face of their anger. The solution is to empower them. Give them action steps toward a resolution and they will feel like they can regain control. The more they feel like they are in the driver's seat, the calmer they will be.

For "frequent flier" customers, it's important to recognize that their codependency stems from insecurity. The more secure you can make them feel, the less they will need you. Teach them to be independent. Give them the tools so they can rely on themselves instead of you. This is the one time I'd make an exception to the rule of never offering outside resources when you have the answer. If it helps them to have a long-term ability to rely on themselves, these tools can be helpful in providing them that independence.

TIP #4: SET LIMITS YOU MUST

While you may be a Customer Service Jedi, you are not super-human. In order to keep your patience intact, you must learn to set limits so you can avoid an impatient outburst. Part of setting those limits means taking breaks when you need them.

Here are a few scary statistics reported in a survey about the North American 'work break' culture[4]:

1. Almost 20% of North American employees worry about taking lunch breaks because they believe their bosses will pass negative judgment on their work ethic.
2. 22% of North American bosses believe

employees who take a regular lunch break are less hardworking.

3. Overall, 38% of employees don't feel their workplaces encourage lunch breaks.

According to this survey, 90% of employees feel revitalized by breaks. Breaks not only improve mental health, but also increase productivity. I include these statistics to give you permission to ask for and take breaks because, in the end, it will improve your performance. Even though setting your limits may mean you spend less time engaging with your customers, it will heighten the quality of your interactions and improve the reputation of your company.

Beyond breaks, time management in general is fundamental when it comes to setting your limits. With that in mind, here are some time management techniques worth practicing:

1. Discuss with your superiors about implementing a firm deadline for your workday to end. This means that if your call center closes at 5 PM, you don't want your workday to also end at 5 PM. This could lead to the situation of the 4:59 PM caller who extends your workday. Instead, try to find a happy medium with your company. If your workday is set to end at 5 PM, your call center should close at 4:30 PM. This way, you have time to wrap up any lingering calls without anxiety. This doesn't mean you're wasting the last 30 minutes. If you're not wrapping up calls,

you can spend the remaining 30 minutes doing other work such as following up on emails. Talking to a supervisor about changing strategy can be intimidating, but if your suggestion improves agent-customer relations, your superiors will also reap the benefits.

2. Avoid calls with time limits if possible. I realize some employees are put in the position of having to keep calls short, especially if answers are typically straightforward. However, for more complex issues time limits create an environment of anxiety. It's challenging not to make a customer feel like 'just another number' when the clock is ticking.

3. Putting a customer on hold or even calling a customer back the next day are options. As long as you reassure the customer that they have been heard and follow up with them at your soonest convenience, they will generally be understanding.

4. Give yourself the time to learn what you need to learn. As with any job, part of customer service is learning. You need to have patience with yourself so you can take time to research the latest products, trends, and directions of your company. That is part of the job and it's ok to use work time to improve your knowledge in these arenas.

TIP #5: ALONE YOU ARE NOT

When your patience is pushed to its limits, remember that you are not alone. You have colleagues. You have managers. You have bosses. There are people around whom you can reach out to before you snap. Of course, if you can be your customer's sole point of contact that is always preferable, but that doesn't mean you can't enlist the assistance of your co-workers to help you find a solution more quickly and efficiently.

THE OBI-WANS OF CUSTOMER SERVICE: MANAGERS, TRAINERS, BUSINESS OWNERS

"If you define yourself by the power to take life, the desire to dominate, to possess...then you have nothing."

— *OBI-WAN KENOBI*

Managers, business owners, and trainers are the ones who set a precedent for patience in the workplace. This means that if a customer service agent is impatient, their manager holds partial responsibility.

How can managers avoid having impatient agents? Follow these steps you must:

Model Patience

The reciprocity principle for patience we discussed earlier in the chapter does not only apply to agent and customer interactions, it also applies to interactions with your employees. Be patient as they are learning, be patient when they are frustrated, and be patient when they make mistakes. You and your customers will receive patience back in return.

If you have trouble cultivating patience with frustrating employees, exercise empathy. Would you want to receive a call at 4:59 PM? Most likely not. Empathy breeds patience and patience breeds understanding.

Set the Environment for Patience

Managers have to lay the foundation for employees to have patience. If your employees are constantly pushed to their breaking point, they will break. A few tips to set the right environment:

- Have regular breaks for your employees and make sure they feel encouraged to take those breaks.
- Give your employees time at the end of the day to wrap up their affairs so they are not rushing their customers through that 4:59 PM call.
- Unless it is absolutely necessary, avoid imposing short time limits for calls. Some callers will need more time than others. An agent should not be merited primarily on their ability to quickly get the caller off the phone in less than 2 minutes.
- Make sure you are sufficiently staffed. There is no need to overburden your employees. The cost of poor customer service will outweigh the benefit of a greater volume of calls taken per agent.
- Give your employees the necessary tools and training before taking calls. Don't throw them into the water too early or they will sink.
- Have plenty of available resources for your customers to find answers on their own: videos, articles, classes, etc. The more answers you have

available, the less burden you will put on your customer service representatives.

By following these steps, you'll not only improve the customer-agent relationship, but you'll also build your company's reputation and ultimately lead to more sales. Calls might be longer and you may have to invest more in staffing upfront, but this investment in your employee satisfaction will lead to greater productivity and better service.

Hire the Right People

Sometimes you can set the right environment and be the shining example of patience yourself, but your employees won't follow your lead. That's why it's important to hire the right people. Don't just look for a body to fill a seat when hiring, use patience as a litmus test for your customer service agents. Do they show patience in their interview?

Remember: An agent is a representative of your business. What your customer feels about your agent, they will most likely feel about your business as a whole. Your customer service team is the spirit of your company. Choose wisely you must. At the end of this book I'll share some bonus tips on how to hire the right people.

Whether you are an agent, a manager, or an entrepreneur, I hope this chapter has impressed upon you the vitality of patience. And remember, you can sometimes find patience by keeping in mind what you're here to do: Help people. Returning to that core purpose during challenging times can make patience possible.

"The best way to pursue happiness is to help other people. Nothing else will make you happier."

— GEORGE LUCAS

PILLAR TWO:

UNDERSTANDING

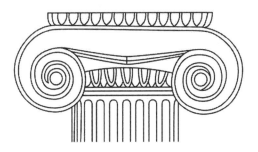

PILLAR TWO: UNDERSTANDING

The Secret of Stellar Service Representatives

Bill called my line one day while I was working as a customer service representative in IT. He asserted that he was a bit of a tech whiz (if he did say so himself). However, for the life of him, he could not access his product subscription page on our website.

Taking Bill at his word regarding his self-proclaimed digital prowess, I asked him to tell me each step he took and describe the specific error he was seeing.

He recited the correct steps and, when he got to the product page, it *should* have opened. But it didn't. Techie Bill didn't understand. And neither did I. So I asked him to repeat each step while I was on the phone with him.

I had a perturbed Bill walk me through the steps one by one. He balked at the task saying, "I just told you this!" To which I reassured him, "You did, but let's do it again together."

As we went through the steps, Bill reasserted that he was, in fact, tech-savvy. At one point, he even chastised me with, "If you are going to tell me to reset my router or clear my cache in my browser, I did that before calling you. You obviously have an inferior site."

Just as I was getting ready to offer credit for the missed access time, I finally understood! I hadn't checked whether Bill was using the correct browser to access his subscription page.

At the time, my company's product page could only be opened using Chrome. We specified this fact to our subscribers prior to their purchase.

"As you know, Bill, our site only works in Chrome. Let's confirm that we are using Chrome."

"Of course I am!" he exclaimed.

"I hear you," I said with as much compassion as I could muster. "I am aware you know your way around technology. Let's make sure your browser didn't change itself on you."

I asked Bill to describe what he saw on his screen. Lo and behold, I was able to identify from his description that he was *not* using the correct browser. We found out that, unbeknownst to Bill, his default browser had changed from Chrome to Safari. Once we identified the issue, Bill opened the subscription page on Chrome with zero issues.

At the end of the call, we had found a resolution and Bill left as a satisfied customer. The secret that made this interaction work was understanding.

WHAT IS UNDERSTANDING AND WHY DO WE NEED IT?

Welcome to "U" University. In this chapter, we'll explore Pillar Two, aka the "U" in P.U.R.E., which stands for **understanding**.

In Pillar One, we learned that patience is the foundation on which a good customer service experience is built. With patience, you learn to be present, stay in touch with the temperature of the moment, and hold space for your customer to get what they need out of the call.

Keeping that foundation of patience in mind, we can now build on it with a layer of understanding.

While patience enables you to tune into your customer's *feelings*, understanding is the *mental* component that bridges your roles as a sounding board, teacher, and savior. With understanding, you are not only prepared to receive your customer in an empathetic way, but you are also able to assess their intent and provide a solution based on that intent. In other words, you put yourself in your customer's shoes and walk with them between the problem and the resolution.

To demonstrate understanding in the context of a customer service call would sound something like this:

"_____ is what I heard you're having trouble with, and _____ is how we will resolve this issue."

Understanding may seem like it should just be common sense, but there are three trends that convince me understanding is no longer intuitive:

1. The growing disconnect between customer

service representatives and their customers due
to automated response machines.

2. The rise of individualism.
3. The decline of empathy.

A foundational ability to understand others is no longer
a given for many people. This was apparent in my own
observations while training customer service
representatives to connect with their customers. It
became obvious many of my trainees had never
developed the ability to 'put themselves in another
person's shoes.' It was a lesson I took for granted
because I learned it as a little girl.

As a society, we've become so individually focused that
understanding is now a challenging and tiresome mental
exercise instead of an instinctive reaction. When society
leans towards social division and identity preservation,
the muscles of understanding are either underdeveloped
or have atrophied.

These observations are not simply the gripes of
someone echoing a 'back in the good ol' days' sentiment.
The rise of individualism and decline in empathy is
actually strongly supported by scientific research.
Consider these studies:

1. In 2017, a team of researchers analyzed the
   incidence of individualism in 78 countries over a
   51-year period and found that it has increased by
   about 12 percent worldwide since 1960.[1]
2. A 2011 study[2] examined self-reported rates of
   empathy among college students over a 30-year
   period and discovered a drastic decline in

empathy starting in the early 2000's. Nearly 75% of modern participants rated themselves as *less empathetic* than the average student did 30 years prior. It is no surprise that the rates of self-reported narcissism concurrently skyrocketed during this time.

Teaching the concept of understanding *is* necessary in today's world. Our modern world does not give us the basic tools to make understanding easy. However, we are all born with the *ability* to understand, even if many of us don't exercise this muscle on a day-to-day basis.

The fact that you are reading this book means you are willing to grow in your ability to understand others! Hopefully you can take that as a kernel of encouragement as we dive in. Without customer service agents who possess the ability to understand, a business is all but sure to fail.

Since understanding is a mental exercise, let's lean on a few insights from some of the world's greatest minds to help guide us on this journey of **understanding**.

We'll start with this quote from English philosopher John Locke,

"The improvement of understanding is for two ends: First, for our own increase of knowledge; second, for enabling us to deliver that knowledge to others."

In other words, the process of understanding is two-fold:

Step 1: Acquire knowledge.

Step 2: Impart knowledge unto others.

Considering John Locke's wise words, we'll divide this chapter into two sections: the *Art of Gaining Knowledge* and the *Art of Sharing Knowledge*. At the end of the chapter you'll get a few words of wisdom about the common enemies of understanding, as well as some additional advice for managers, business owners, and trainers.

GAINING KNOWLEDGE

There are two types of knowledge you'll need to gain as a customer service representative. First there is your preparation *before* interacting with your customers. Then there is the quest for knowledge *during* the interaction. Let's examine these one at a time.

BEFORE THE INTERACTION

Before you even pick up the phone or greet a customer, you should do three things:

1. Learn about your product
2. Cultivate the right mindset
3. Take ownership of your role

1. Learn about your product

"You do not really understand something unless you can explain it to your grandmother."
-Albert Einstein

Understanding your product means you not only *know* information about it, but you can competently *teach* that information to others (remember, one of your customer service roles *is* as a teacher). Unless your grasp on the design and use of your product is thorough enough that you could explain it to your 96-year-old grandmother, you do not know it well enough.

This requires more work than taking a basic training course, reading the user manual, and looking up the product details. Start by doing those things, but then take your learning a step further. Once you know how your product or service works, figure out how it doesn't work.

Part of understanding is learning how something breaks.

Most of the time, customers will not be calling to praise your company or product. Rather, they need assistance. The product or service is not meeting their expectations, and they want you to right whatever is wrong.

Use the product yourself and try to make it malfunction. Then, find a way to resolve the issue. Learn what errors your customers *could* encounter so you can guide them to the resolutions when they *do*.

I used this strategy with immense success back in the early 90's when the first touch screen ATMs came out. At the time I was working for a major bank in the customer service department. These ATMs had a phone line attached with a direct dial to our customer service line. This ATM technology was brand new, and people were leery about using it, so we wanted to make sure our support team was right there to help.

As a customer service agent, I wanted to do my best to ease people into this novel system. So I found a touchscreen ATM machine and did my best to learn how it worked. I spent hours trying to make every mistake I possibly could. By the end of this learning process, I could identify what a customer did wrong simply by listening to the tones of the buttons they pressed. In fact, the customers I helped were so impressed they often asked, "Can you see me?" A few customers even brought friends back to show them what I could do.

By undergoing this learning process, I was able to relate to my customers as a guide who had been there, done that, and knew the pathway to resolution.

2. Cultivating the Right Mindset

"Alone we can do so little; together we can do so much."
-Helen Keller

Remember Bill from the beginning of this chapter? Did anything stand out to you in the way I described my interaction with Bill? Take, for example, this statement:

"We found out that, unbeknownst to Bill, his default browser had changed from Chrome to Safari. Once we identified the issue, Bill opened the subscription page on Chrome with zero issues."

The key here: *"We"*

"We found out..."

"*We* identified the issue..."

Understanding is a collaborative endeavor. In order to set the stage for receiving knowledge from your customer, you must recognize that you and your customer have the same goal in mind.

Last chapter, we talked about thinking of your customer as your ally. In this chapter, I'm going to ask you to take that mindset a step further.

Think of your customer like a **teammate**.

Either you both succeed or you both fail. You are not trying to prove your customer wrong, you are simply trying to get to the bottom of an issue together.

When I spoke to Bill, my reaction wasn't, "See, Bill, I was right! You *aren't* using Chrome." It was, "I'm glad *we* could resolve this issue together."

In another instance, a customer service agent I was training was dealing with a customer who was locked out of her account. In order to resolve the issue, the customer had to log out of one of the devices she was currently logged into. But she could not remember which other devices were logged in. My trainee said, "Well, you better figure out where you logged in or you'll be locked out forever."

While my trainee wasn't wrong in his assessment, he was wrong in the way he approached the customer. By shifting responsibility onto the customer, he voided the team alliance. A better way for the representative to approach this would have been to say: "I need you to do your best to remember where you last logged into. Unfortunately, we cannot resolve this issue without that information." By using the royal "we" even when the customer is the only one with access to the information, you remind the customer that you are on their team working with them toward a win.

By adopting a "we" mindset before you even pick up the phone, you set the stage for understanding.

3. Owning Your Role

"People ask the difference between a leader and a boss. The leader leads, and the boss drives." -Theodore Roosevelt

Now that we've established you and your customer are a team, it's important to recognize your role on that team. As a customer service advocate, your role is a **team leader**.

You are tasked with gathering the knowledge that will bring you and your customer to victory. You are not a taskmaster. Being a good team leader means taking responsibility for the success of your teammates. You should be thinking, "What information do I need, and what information does my customer need to use the product better or fix the issue?"

Your customer is not your only teammate. Any available co-worker who can help you find a resolution is also a teammate. Your business as a whole is your teammate. It's vital that, in the eyes of the customer, you present a united front.

Recently, I ran into an issue with a representative I was training. When a customer would complain about the way a product worked,

the rep would say something like, "Oh, I'm sorry *they* designed it that way."

When you disassociate yourself from your company like this, you imply that your company is separate from you. Remember, to your customer; you are the face of your company. You are a part of that company. A better way to respond in that situation would be, "We designed this product to work in this fashion, let's work together to see how we can make the product work for you."

As I've said before, you should be your customer's sole point of contact if possible. But this does not mean you need to disassociate yourself from your team. Even if you will not be working on the direct resolution to your customer's problem you still need to act as the team leader.

If a customer calls in about an issue with their network disconnecting avoid saying, "The network team will take care of this for you," because that puts a degree of separation between you and the resolution. It shows a divided ship to your customer, who might think, "Why am I not talking directly to the network team? How do I get in touch with them?"

The customer needs to know that you see a direct path to the desired end result. Even if someone else is feeding you the answers, it's important your customer knows you are the person who is going to help them. So, instead of telling the customer, "The network team will take care of it," approach the customer by saying, "My team and I will take care of it."

DURING THE INTERACTION

The previous section examined how to gather the knowledge you need to help customers before you ever pick up a phone. Next, let's talk about what to do during the call when your focus should be on acquiring the necessary knowledge to solve the problem directly from the customer. In order to gain this knowledge, follow four basic rules:

1. Listen with intention
2. Echo with empathy
3. Clarify with curiosity
4. Learn with humility

1. Listen With Intention

"If you make listening and observation your occupation, you will gain much more than you can by talk." -Robert Baden-Powell

The key to gaining knowledge during a call is listening.

Just as listening is a pivotal part of patience, listening is also an important aspect in understanding.

However, listening in order to understand means more than just being receptive to the information at hand. It means also becoming a detective to uncover the customer's true intent.

When we discussed *active* listening in the last chapter, I said:

"When you are truly listening, you will hear not only what is being said, but what is not being said."

Let's explore how you can listen for what is and is not being said.

The best way to listen with intention is to pay attention to the visual, verbal, and tonal cues.

Cues can indicate a difference between what the customer is saying and their true intent. Often, recognizing these dissonances can lead you to uncover deeper issues and concerns.

Is your customer saying they want to cancel their membership but expressing hesitation when you talk about benefits of the service?

Does the customer say everything is working fine, but their tone implies they are angry?

Is your customer saying, "No, I absolutely did not break my toaster, it broke on its own!" but fidgeting and averting their gaze?

Picking up on cues is a nuanced process, but the more you deal with customers, the more you will learn to recognize the cues that indicate a disconnect between what they are saying and their true intent.

One afternoon, a woman called in to say she was upset with the quality of her service plan with my company. During her rant she said, almost as an afterthought, "And I don't even understand the billing." I picked up on that small detail and asked her to explain what she meant.

The lightbulb moment came when she said, "I don't understand why my friend is paying less than I am."

Bingo. Let people talk enough and they'll tell you what you need to know. Thank you, patience.

By letting my customer talk, asking the right questions, and listening with intention to uncover clues, I discovered the real issue: the customer wanted to pay less.

With this newfound knowledge, I offered to investigate her friend's plan and compare it to hers. It turned out her friend was on a different plan with a different company, but she couldn't provide me any further details. In the end, the customer simply wanted to leave our service for the greener grass on the other side of the fence. Some people you just have to let go. That said, I learned something very important: Our competitor was offering lower rates. Now that was an important discovery. More on that in a bit.

2. Echo With Empathy

"Empathy has no script. There is no right way or wrong way to do it. It's simply listening, holding space, withholding judgment, emotionally connecting, and communicating that incredibly healing message of 'You're not alone.'"
-Brené Brown

Trust is one of the most valuable tools in the patience toolkit. Trust not only disables a customer's defenses, but it also allows them to feel comfortable sharing necessary information.

One quick way to build trust is via empathy. Remember that customers often react with frustrated ramblings or angry tirades when they feel their problem isn't being heard. You can make your customer feel heard by echoing them with empathy.

This means acknowledging the issue they are facing and responding with a statement that ensures you understand their predicament from both an intellectual perspective as well as an emotional one. People want to know that someone sees how they feel and that their feelings matter. Empathetic statements assure your customer that they are not alone in their predicament.

While you should never be reading directly from a script, there are a few timeless phrases you can use to show empathy:

"You're making total sense."

"I understand how you feel."

"You're in a tough spot here."

"I can feel the frustration you feel."

"I wish you didn't have to go through that."

"That must be so hard for you."

As you progress through your career, build upon this list with your own key phrases that you can reference when dealing with customers.

When you are dealing with a customer over the phone, your tonality impacts the perception of empathy. Just consider the phrase, "I'm fine." It can either be a straightforward assertion or a thinly veiled threat, depending on circumstance. Be sure that you give your customer the right tone to convey empathy. The words alone are not enough.

While it is important to empathize with a customer's feelings, be wary of outright agreeing with them. You still need to do the necessary work to uncover the heart of their issue before indulging their assessment of the situation.

Empathy does not excuse you from due diligence.

3. Clarify With Curiosity

"Knowing where you came from is no less important than knowing where you are going." -Neil Degrasse Tyson

Part of gathering information for understanding is ensuring that the information you are collecting gives you an accurate picture of the situation. I think of this as a three-step process.

Step 1: Use probing questions to get to the root of the issue.

Step 2: Reaffirm the issue.

Step 3: If necessary, repeat steps already taken by the customer.

In Step 1, it is important to ask quality, investigative questions that will allow you to garner specific details from the customer. As I mentioned in the previous chapter, the real crux of an issue is usually hiding under several questions.

A friend of mine once called Amazon in fury because she had purchased a movie and it didn't show up in her library. She thought Amazon had ripped her off. Although the Amazon customer service agent empathized with her, they did not immediately agree with my friend's conclusion. Instead, they asked her a few specific, probing questions such as, "Which account are you currently signed into?"

It turned out she was signed into her kid's account. Go figure.

Simple, specific questions can yield critical clarifications. Without these questions, my friend and the agent may have been unnecessarily engaged in a 30 minute phone call figuring out a 2 minute issue.

One important note: Asking a series of seemingly mundane or repetitive questions can begin to feel like an interrogation for a customer. If your customer starts to get frustrated, empathetically remind them you are asking these questions for their benefit. Try something like:

"I know it's frustrating to answer these questions. Thank you for your patience. I'm asking because I want to ensure we are thorough so we can find the best resolution for this issue."

After you've asked your questions, it's time to proceed to Step 2: Reaffirmation.

Using reaffirmation ensures mutual understanding. It doesn't do you any good to gather information if you don't make sure it is correct. Here are a few examples of reaffirming phrases:

"To be sure I'm taking you in the right direction, is correct?"

"Okay, I think I get it. So what I'm hearing is..."

"Let me paraphrase and summarize what you're saying. You're saying..."

By reaffirming, you make sure you are both on the same page, and you provide reassurance for your customer that you understand what they are saying. Even if you're not entirely certain of the customer's issue, it's important to repeat what you've learned so far in the conversation instead of using an accusatory statement or generalized question to clarify. Phrases such as, "You're not explaining yourself properly," "I don't get what you're saying," or, "What do you mean?" can imply that you aren't paying attention to your customer. When you repeat what you see as the issue, even if it's only part of the story, the customer automatically knows you have been listening.

On to Step 3. If necessary, you may need to run the customer through the motions again to ensure they have done it correctly.

A pivotal part of understanding is knowing where you came from. That can sometimes mean literally walking through an issue with a customer so you can see exactly what they saw when they first had the issue.

As someone who has worked in the IT sector for a long time, this can be particularly important to do when it comes to resolving a technological issue. The old adage, "Doing the same thing again and expecting different results is the definition of insanity," is not necessarily accurate in the tech industry. In technology, sometimes the same process can yield a different result.

Remember Bill from the beginning of this chapter? If we hadn't gone through each of the steps, we would not have been able to identify that he was using the incorrect browser. Yes, this can be frustrating for your customer. Reassure them that you are repeating the steps for their benefit so you can find a resolution together.

4. Learn from Your Customer

"Experience is a master teacher, even when it's not our own."
-Gina Greenlee

Remember the customer who was upset with her service because she found out her friend was paying less than her?

Not only did I learn what she was truly struggling with in the course of the call, but I also discovered our competitor was offering a lower rate than my company. Instead of getting angry about this newfound knowledge, I recognized I could use this information to either lower my rate or ensure I was offering enough value to justify the higher price tag.

As a representative, try as you might to prepare yourself for anything a customer might say, you will never have a 100% success rate. Customers will identify issues with your product or service that you and your company are unaware of.

How should you react?

First, be sure to thank your customer. It's tempting to make excuses or feel embarrassed, but that would defeat the purpose of the team mentality. You and your customer are in this together! They made a brilliant discovery that can help inform and improve your business. For every person who calls in with an issue, there are another 80 who had the same issue and didn't call. Eventually, those people may give up on the company and the product. That one customer is the person who could be saving you from losing those others.

Second, if you have it within your ability, you should reward that customer. A free month's subscription to your service? Some free swag? Exclusive access to a cool video? When you reward a customer who gives you new information, you acknowledge their part in developing your business. To boot, when you give them a reward they're also more likely to tell their friends about how you treated them. Word of mouth for the win!

Third, use the knowledge you gained. Take it to your company and tell your team how you could use your client's discovery to fix an issue, and dig deeper into the insight so you can be more prepared to help future customers. This brings us to the invaluable art of sharing knowledge.

SHARING KNOWLEDGE

Once you've learned about your product and gained the necessary knowledge from your customer, it's time to teach your customer how to fix the problem.

Don't let anyone tell you teaching is easy. Explaining a complex or foreign subject can be challenging under the best of circumstances. The problem is that the other person is not in your head. While the knowledge might seem obvious to you, it may not be so clear to others.

Humans have a bias toward believing our personal knowledge is common knowledge. In 1990, a Standard University study illustrated this exact point [3] The researcher had subjects play a game in which they would "tap out" the rhythm of common songs such as "Happy Birthday" or "Row Row Row, Your Boat" on a table. Another person in the room then tried to guess what songs they were tapping out.

During the experiment, 120 songs were tapped out. The average "tapper" believed the listener would guess correctly 50% of the time. But the actual success rate was just 2.5%.

My friend Karen came to visit me shortly after she got married. At the time, she was unsatisfied in her relationship because she believed her husband wasn't being understanding. After we talked about her marriage, she launched into a story about how she ran into a friend at the grocery store. I couldn't understand why this new story was relevant, but Karen was still speaking in the same impassioned tone. Midway through her story I was so lost I stopped Karen in her tracks. "Karen," I said, "I hear this is important to you, but I'm not in your head. Help me understand."

You could see the lightbulb click behind her eyes.

The next day, Karen's husband Barney came to visit me. "You just saved my marriage," he said. He had been trying in vain to articulate to his wife that he was not understanding her stories because he could not figure out how they were relevant.

In the end, the remedy was simple: Refine the explanation. Karen understood that while she knew the details, her husband didn't. She got better at explaining and, consequently, her husband got better at understanding.

To make sure you explain something properly, follow this process:

Step 1: Gain permission from your customer to explain

Step 2: Assure your customer you can lead them to resolution

Step 3: Establish a game plan

Step 4: Explain

STEP 1: Gaining Permission

"No man is good enough to govern another man without the other's consent."
-Abraham Lincoln

Before starting any explanation, it is important that you gain permission from your customer to proceed toward a solution. This shows you respect your customer enough to ask for their consent and establishes a baseline of trust. It makes them feel comfortable that you will not do anything without their consent. For example,

"I'm so sorry you're going through this experience. I have a solution for you. Are you ready to hear it?"

By gaining permission to proceed, you let your customer feel in control.

It is important to phrase this request in the form of a yes or no question. This not only sets a precedent for your customer to say "yes" to your future requests, it also makes them feel like they are in the driver's seat. Should they need to stop the process at any time, they know they are able to do so.

STEP 2: Reassuring

> *"Leadership is an action, not a position."*
> *-Donald McGannon*

Reassuring your customer that you are on their side and working toward a solution is critical to establishing the trust needed to guide them to fix the problem. When your customer trusts that you have their best interest in mind, they will be more open to actively working with you toward a solution. Set the stage for this trust by starting your explanation with an empowered statement. This helps communicate that you will be able to lead them toward resolution.

"I can assure you that I can help you."

"Working together, we will handle this."

"Let's take the steps to get the results you want."

STEP 3: Establishing a Game Plan

"You take people as far as they will go, not as far as you would like them to go."
-Jeanette Rankin

After you've gained permission and reassured your customer that you are the one who can lead them to resolution, it's time to lay out your plan of action. This is also a good point to circle back and get your customer's contact information if you haven't already. You don't want to establish a bond of trust with your customer only to lose them due to a faulty phone connection. Make sure your customer has a lifeline back to you so you can reconnect if necessary. Once that lifeline is secure, you can establish a game plan with your customer.

Lay out the path to resolution. You want to prepare your customer for what is to come. Set expectations for timeline and the level of participation required from them. By laying out the game plan, you'll enable your customer to pinpoint where the gaps are. So, if you specify, "This process will take 20 minutes," your customer could respond, "I only have 5 minutes." By identifying the requirements of the process at the outset, you avoid the frustration of mismatched expectations.

As you lay out the timeline and action steps, make sure you keep getting permission before proceeding so your customer feels like they are in control.

For example, imagine you are investigating a fraudulent charge. It takes 5 days to investigate and a temporary charge will be placed on a customer's account for 2 days as a test. But maybe the customer has a mortgage payment that will be withdrawn from their account in the next 2 days and the temporary charge could result in an overdraw. If you did not gain permission for this procedure and simply implemented the course of action, it could result in an added financial burden on your customer. However, if you make them aware at the outset of the procedure, they can either give you permission to proceed or they can halt the investigation until they are better prepared.

Further, if you notice during the process that it is taking longer than anticipated, or requires more from your customer than you expressed at the outset, make sure to re-check in with them.

"We've been on the phone for 20 minutes, I just wanted to check-in to make sure you are alright proceeding. Most likely, a resolution will take about 10 more minutes. Shall we continue?"

STEP 4: Explaining

> *"Everything is complicated if no one explains it to you."*
> *-Fredrik Backman*

Let's assume your customer has agreed to proceed with your plan of action. Congratulations! Now comes the actual explanation toward resolution. When explaining, specificity is your knight in shining armor.

Much of the time, the information you need to convey is completely new to your customer and they do not have the benefit of being inside your brain. Here are a few tips to remember for being specific in your explanation:

#1: Limit your use of jargon

I was working in IT when Microsoft Office shifted from their 2003 version to their 2013 edition. At the time, Microsoft started referring to the set of toolbars at the top of their programs as the "ribbon." However, this was not common knowledge among most of our customers. We ran into situations where the customer service representative would say, "Now click the layout tab in your ribbon," and the customers would respond with something akin to, "Ribbon? Like a ribbon that goes in your hair?"

Jargon, even if it is cute, is meaningless if your customer is not also familiar with the language. You're not here to be cute, you're here to be practical. You are not a Louboutin high heel. On the phone with your customer, you are a Croc Clog. Support before style.

#2: Take your time

You are not in a race. Don't rush through the steps only to find a misunderstanding with your customer.

#3: Do regular check-ins

A critical component in mutual understanding is making sure your customer is with you at each step of the process. That way, if you or your customer make a mistake, you can quickly identify where the error occurred. It should go something like this: Complete Step 1. Check in. Complete Step 2. Check in. And so on.

When you check in, make sure you are getting a picture of what they are doing on their side to ensure they are proceeding through each step with you. "Were you able to login to your account?" "Yes." "Do you see the tab that says 'subscription'?" "Yes." "Click on that button."

Hot tip: When possible, stick to questions that elicit a "yes/no" response. This will avoid open-ended answers that could lead you both down a distracting rabbit hole.

#4: Ask your customer to specify during the process

When Bill from the beginning of the chapter was struggling with his subscription and assured me he was using Chrome, I asked him to describe what he saw on his screen. Because he described it, I was able to identify the physical attributes that distinguished the Safari page from the Chrome page and thus clarify that he was not, in fact, on Chrome.

#5: Measure success by result

How do you know at the end of a call whether you've explained yourself well enough? The result. Getting the result you want will tell you whether you've given enough detail to your customer to find resolution.

ENEMIES OF UNDERSTANDING

Are you familiar with *The Four Agreements*[4]? These four agreements are essentially an outline for understanding and happiness. They are as follows:

Agreement 1: Be Impeccable With Your Word

Agreement 2: Don't Take Anything Personally

Agreement 3: Don't Make Assumptions

Agreement 4: Always Do Your Best

Some companies have started incorporating these agreements into their customer service training, and with good reason. By following these four agreements, customer service agents can establish trust and connection with customers.

However, the *enemies* of understanding can also be identified by looking at the antitheses of these four agreements. These enemies are: lack of clarity, judgement, assuming, and giving up. Allow me to embellish...

Enemy #1: Lack of Clarity

"It's a lack of clarity that creates chaos and frustration. Those emotions are poison to any living goal."
-Steve Maraboli

If you do not have clarity—or worse, if you have inauthenticity—then you should prepare for an uphill battle. Being thorough, clear, and truthful is the only path toward understanding.

Enemy #2: Judgement

"Whenever you feel like criticizing anyone...just remember that all the people in this world haven't had the advantages that you've had."
-F. Scott Fitzgerald

There are moments when you are going to judge your customer. Customer service is a strange balance between empathetically guiding your customer toward a result and keeping your personal feelings out of the situation. In those moments where I find it challenging not to judge my customers, I remind myself that the bottom line is I am there to help. And sometimes helping means recognizing they have not led the same life as me. Just as they are not in my head, I am not in theirs.

When I was working in customer service at a bank, a woman called in because her mom had passed away and she needed to cash out the trust account. The first ten minutes of the call were spent helping the woman process her emotions. When she was through, I expressed my condolences and asked if she'd rather resolve the issue at another time. Her tone flipped on a dime. Suddenly, I realized she was desperate to get her hands on this money.

My first thought was, "Wow, you greedy little..." I won't finish that sentence, but it was not a kind thought. However, I checked myself and worked hard to preserve my professionalism and move toward a resolution. As I later found out, the woman was desperate for the money because she was unable to pay her child's college tuition. Without the trust money, her kid would soon be kicked out of university.

In the end, I was not able to accommodate her request for immediate distribution of the funds due to restrictions in our bank policies. She ended up walking away mad, but I walked away with a greater sense of compassion and understanding.

One tip: If you're finding it challenging to disassociate yourself from your feelings, try putting the resolution first. Concentrate on getting to results and the feelings, one way or another, need not be part of the conversation.

Enemy #3: Assuming

"Assess before you Assume."
-Lyle Kwiatkowski

To assume makes an ass out of u and me.

This may be a joke, but when it comes to understanding, it couldn't be more true. When you assume facts about your caller without clarifying, you fall prey to misunderstanding.

Make no mistake about it, assuming is the most formidable enemy of understanding.

If, for example, I had not asked Bill whether he was using Chrome and just assumed on his word that he was, we would never have found a resolution.

Enemy #4: Giving Up

Many of life's failures are people who did not realize how close they were to success when they gave up.
-Thomas Edison

We've all had that one customer who makes us want to give up and run for the hills.

During the call they usually say something to the effect of, "Do you even know what you're doing?" making us respond with something like, "Look, lady, I'm here to help you. You don't want my help? Fine!"

Click.

Whoops! I think the call accidentally dropped. Sorry, not sorry.

That said, it is better to end your day knowing you did your best to help every customer. If you give up prematurely, you face the nagging consequence of knowing you did not do everything you could to come to a mutual understanding. Even if it does not work out and your customer exits the conversation before reaching resolution, you will know the fault does not lie with you.

SIDEBAR TO THE MANAGERS

> *"We all need people who will give us feedback. That's how we improve."*
> *-Bill Gates*

Before concluding this chapter, I'd like to have a small sidebar with the managers, entrepreneurs, and trainers about **understanding**.

As with patience, understanding starts with you. Here are few tips to foster better understanding in your workplace:

#1: Equip your staff with the right tools

In order for staff to be successful during the "gaining knowledge" phase of understanding, they have to be equipped with all the necessary information. This goes beyond manuals and tutorials. Allow them the space and flexibility to play with and break your product or service. This hands on approach creates a more informed representative that is able to handle being that singular point of contact for your customers.

#2: Monitor your customer service agents

Just as customer service agents do regular check-ins with their customers, you should be doing regular check-ins with your agents. See what your agents are having trouble understanding or explaining. It is up to you to see where they're struggling and help them do better. *Hint: When there are multiple agents struggling to understand or explain the same issue, it is time to revise the system.*

#3: Learn from the customers

Is there a more efficient way to resolve an issue? If customers keep running into a problem on your website where they encounter a blank page and they don't understand how to proceed you could ask your developers to put up a temporary page with an error message that explains the situation and redirects the visitor. Allow your customers to be your beta testers because, inevitably, they will break things in ways you never even dreamed of. Learn from them and do your work on the backend to help make a better product or service.

#4: Learn from your customer service agents

Your customer service agents are on the frontline of all issues. Sometimes, they will see things you don't. Ask them about it.

Recently, I was putting together a Standard Operating Procedure on implementing a new ticket submission system to notify agents of customer issues. One of my agents alerted me to a potential issue, "What if there's a work order scheduled, but I change the technician assigned to resolve the issue? Will the new tech get an email to notify them of the assignment?" I thought I had covered all my bases, but this thought had never crossed my mind!

Humility is fundamental to understanding. Be humble enough to acknowledge valuable insights from your teammates and you will grow.

If there's one thing I hope you take away from this chapter, it's this: You are not alone. You, your customers, and your co-workers are all on the same team. Working together toward mutual understanding is the only path to resolution.

"Understanding is the first step to acceptance, and only with acceptance can there be recovery."

— *J.K. ROWLING*

PILLAR THREE:

RESPECT

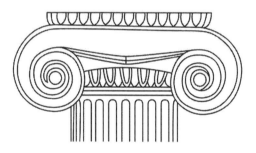

PILLAR THREE: RESPECT

The Third Attribute of Awesome Customer Advocates

R.E.S.P.E.C.T.

Who else has Aretha Franklin in their head right now?

It's difficult to hear this word and not think of the iconic song.

In this chapter, you'll find out what R.E.S.P.E.C.T. means to me. In the spirit of Aretha, we'll explore the concept of respect using a few familiar tunes to guide us along.

So, what *does* respect mean to me? Let's start with a basic definition.

Respect is defined as *"due regard for the feelings, wishes, rights, or traditions of others."*

Like understanding, respect is meant to build upon the previous pillars. Understanding cannot be present without patience, and respect cannot be achieved without a foundation of both patience and understanding.

By now, our study of patience and understanding has hopefully provided you with two fundamental superpowers: 1) the ability to empathize with your customer and 2) a willingness to help your customer.

Let's consider superpower #1 for a moment. Adding respect into this equation, you can put yourself in another person's shoes and *then* take a step back. This results in not only the ability to empathize, but the ability to sympathize.

Sympathy helps you understand someone's perspective and struggles *without* internalizing them. This allows you to connect with your customer while maintaining enough distance from the situation to be able to effectively resolve it. Combine this sympathy with superpower #2, a willingness to help your customer, and it adds up to a day saving **attitude of service**.

Author John C. Maxwell said, "People can hear your words, but they *feel* your attitude."

The right attitude enables you to abide by the platinum rule of respect:

> *Treat the customer __better than__ you want to be treated.*

Why do we need this platinum rule? When it comes to customer service the golden rule of treating others as we would want to be treated isn't enough. We may be more tolerant of certain behaviors that would be unacceptable to other people. Perhaps *you* don't mind being kept on hold for 3 minutes, but customer Carla who is in the middle of managing 4 screaming kids will not feel the same way.

In a famous 1996 study[1] comparing the reaction of men from the Southern U.S. and men from the northern U.S. in response to another man bumping into them and calling them a not-so-nice word, the men from the North were relatively unaffected. The men from the South, on the other hand, perceived this action as a considerable insult and, consequently, were more likely to have an aggressive response. This study shows us that we cannot always predict what will be considered disrespectful to someone. Therefore, it is critical that we take particular care to go beyond simply treating others how we want to be treated.

We should treat them how *they* want to be treated.

"What you want/ Baby, I got it/ What you need/Do you know I got it/All I'm askin'/Is for a little respect..."

— *ARETHA FRANKLIN, RESPECT*

THE SIX ASPECTS OF RESPECT

Respect is less straightforward than patience and understanding. It's challenging to gauge what will be interpreted as respectful or disrespectful. That said, there are steps you can take to ensure a high probability that your actions will be viewed in a positive light:

1. What You Say
2. How You Say It
3. Timing
4. What Your Customer Says
5. Withholding Judgment
6. Owning Your Mistakes

1. WHAT YOU SAY

"Mm, whatcha say?/Mm, that you only meant well?/Well, of course you did." Jason Derulo, Whatcha Say

Although you may *think* your words convey respect, your customer might wind up with a different impression. That is, your customer may not buy whatever you are trying to sell. Literally or figuratively.

Choosing the right words will help create a sense of familiarity and ease. When combined with the other qualities of respect such as how you *say* those words, this action will help to cultivate a trusting relationship between you and your customer.

By now, you should have a basic comprehension of the right words to say to a customer to demonstrate patience and understanding. A quick reminder:

• When possible, use the person's name instead of "Sir" or "Ma'am". This shows that you view them as a person, not a number.
• For the same reason, use terms like "you" and "I".

- Ask permission to proceed to make them feel like they have a choice.
- Be transparent and clear in your instructions toward resolution.
- Asking probing questions to demonstrate your awareness of and interest in their unique situation.
- Don't over-use jargon.
- Do not over-explain.

To show respect to your customers you need to meet them where they are at. Use your **attitude of service** to empathize with their position, cater to what they need in that moment, and usher them toward a resolution.

Jargon and over-explaining are the two most common roadblocks to showing respect. While the other aforementioned ways of verbally demonstrating respect are straightforward, these two factors are more ambiguous. What can be jargon to one person may be matter-of-fact to another.

If someone calls in about how to use the "Labels" function in Microsoft Office Word you may start by saying, "In the mailings tab in the ribbon, you'll see a button that says 'label.'" But the customer might have no clue what a ribbon even is. By using jargon without explanation, you've made her feel inept...and no one wants to feel inept.

Alternatively, you could say, "Now, do you see on your computer, the little blue picture that has a "W" on it? Click that to open up Word." While this might work for a confused 96-year-old granny, if you're dealing with a 25-year-old accounting executive, this over-explanation could give them the impression that you are a condescending dillweed.

You must assess on a case-by-case basis which type of explanation someone needs. A good rule of thumb is to avoid jargon altogether unless the customer introduces it first. If jargon is essential to your explanation, ask the customer whether they are familiar with the term. If they are not, give them a simple, clear explanation. If they are, believe them and move on. No need to test your customer on their knowledge once they've confirmed they are familiar with something. Testing your customer will only demonstrate that you do not respect *their* words.

2. HOW YOU SAY IT

"If I listen to your lies, would you say/I'm a man (a man) without conviction/I'm a man (a man) who doesn't know/How to sell (to sell) a contradiction/You come and go, you come and go."-Culture Club, Karma Chameleon

How you say something is arguably *more* important than what you say. When there is a contradiction between how something is said and what is said, people most often trust the way a message is delivered - above the words themselves.

A famous 1971 book penned by Professor of Psychology Dr. Albert Mehrabian confirmed this notion. Dr. Mehrabian's research showed that the *tone* and *facial expression* are more influential on perception than the words said. He concluded that what a person says only accounts for 7% of how a listener perceives the speaker. Conversely, 38% of that perception is based on the tone in which a person said it. The remaining 55% of perception is determined by the speaker's facial expression. When there is inconsistency between the three factors, we get confused[2]

I'll expand on Dr. Mehrabian's research and say, in my own experience, not only are tone and facial expression important, but pace is critical as well. With these three elements, you can either make someone feel like they are a 2-year-old, an imbecile, or an equal. Always aim to make them feel equal.

Tonality

When it comes to your tone of voice, it's important to sound supportive without being overly indulgent.

For example, you *should* make a verbal acknowledgement when customers have taken steps toward resolution, but you don't want to say it in a way that puts them on an uncomfortably high pedestal for performing a menial task.(E.g. Complimenting them in the tone of "Oh! What a good customer you are!" as if you're talking to your 2 year old who has just peed in the potty for the first time. This is awkward for everyone involved.)

Another important aspect of cultivating a respectful tone is ensuring that when you check in with your customer you use questions and phrases that leave little room for misinterpretation. For example, with questions such as, "Do you understand?" it is easy for a customer to misperceive your tone for being judgmental. The same is true for questions such as, "Does that make sense?" With those two questions, in my experience, there is about a 50/50 chance that your customer will misinterpret what you are saying based on their perception of your tone.

A better approach would be to ask a fact-finding question such as, "Do you have any questions about what I said?" This leaves little room for misinterpretation. The very wording of these questions conveys that you assume your customer understands unless they tell you otherwise. This type of question has about a 90% success rate.

Pace

The speed of people's speech indicates whether they perceive themselves to be above or below you in rank. Think for a moment about how you would explain the process of tying your shoes to your 4-year-old-nephew. Now, think of how you would explain to your boss about a quarterly decline in the volume of customer calls you received. One is slow, the other is fast.

In the context of customer service, if a customer calls in from Oklahoma City speaking in short, slow sentences and you answer the phone talking a mile a minute, they might perceive you as anxiously rushing them through the call. On the other hand, if you get a wordy, fast-talker from New York City on the line and you reply to them with the pace of your Oklahoma City caller, they might respond to you with something along the lines of, "Why are you talking so slow? What, do you think I'm stupid or something?"

For pace to be perceived as respectful, the goal is to mirror the caller's speech patterns. This will make them feel like your equal. When you pick up the phone, observe the pace at which your customer is speaking and try to speak at a similar speed. Generally, this method absolves you from too much guesswork. However, be aware that if you are working in a call center with a high volume of calls, you will need to ensure you do the mirror and match process for *each individual customer*.

When I was working in a property management office, back-to-back calls were the norm. One day, I received a call from a customer who was a native English speaker. I slowed down my pace so she could clearly hear and interpret my words. At the end of the call she expressed immense gratitude that someone had taken the time to slow down and enable her to understand without judging her for the language barrier.

As soon as I hung up the phone, it immediately rang again. Fresh off my call with the previous customer, when I answered the new call I was sure to speak slowly and clearly.

"So, your said name is Bob? B-O-B, correct?"

"What's wrong with you?" he responded. "How many ways can you spell Bob? Are you slow?"

Lesson learned. You have to meet the customer where they're at...and that means following their lead.

A small note: While the "mirror and match" principle pertains to pace, it does *not* pertain to aggravation level. So, while I sped up my speech to match Bob, I did not match his irritation.

The one exception to this "mirror and match rule" of pace is that if your customer is talking quickly because they are anxious or upset, you can use a slower pace combined with a lower tone of voice to help calm them down. In these instances, a slower pace is generally perceived as a more level-headed approach.

Facial Expression and Body Language

While most of this book is directed at people who are working in customer service over the phone, facial expression and body language still matter.

Even though Dr. Mehrabian's research only looked at facial expressions, body language can also convey respect. If you are assisting someone in person or over a virtual platform such as Zoom, be sure your expression and body language matches your intent. Refer back to Pillar One on Patience for a list of traits such as steady eye contact, nodding your head, angling your body toward your customer, and not fidgeting. These behaviors will indicate that you are with your customer and you respect them enough to give them your full attention.

One last comment on *how* you communicate: As was the case with jargon, you will be walking a fine line of interpretation. Your customer may misunderstand your tone or facial expression. You may not get it right and that's ok. It happens to all of us. There will always be those 2-5% of people who are going to be offended no matter what you say or how you say it. Some people start a conversation angry and are determined to stay that way. More on dealing with these types of customers at the end of the chapter..

3. TIMING

"In a New York Minute, everything can change." - Don Henley, New York Minute

For most people, time is a precious commodity. In today's ever-changing world, many of us are on the run from the moment our alarm clocks ring. People care about how their time is monopolized by others, particularly when it involves an unpleasant task. When we feel our time has been abused, we feel disrespected and are likely to lash out.

As a customer service representative, the onus falls on you to keep your customer informed about *how* and *why* you are spending their time. Always do your best to ensure you are not wasting your customer's time unnecessarily.

We'll divide this section into two important elements of time that impact a customer's perception of respect: hold time and follow-up time.

Hold Time

For most customers, hold time is frustrating. While you as a service representative may not have control over the length of hold time before a customer gets on the line with you, you *do* have the ability to manage hold time after your initial conversation.

In order to show respect to your customer when putting them on hold, follow these steps:

- **Ask permission.** When you ask permission to put a customer on hold, you give them the *choice* of how to spend their time. A simple way to phrase this might be, "Is it ok if I put you on hold?" If they say no, offer to follow up at a more convenient time.

- **Be transparent.** Before placing a customer on hold, clarify *what* you are doing, *why* you are doing it, and *how much time* it will take. This reassures your customer that you are actively working on their issue.

- **If the hold time is longer than estimated, check back in with your customer**. This shows you are aware their time is valuable. Apologize for the inconvenience and explain why the hold is taking longer than anticipated. "Sorry for the wait, Bob. I'm still with you, I'm just waiting for the information to load on the computer. It seems our internet is lagging at the moment." *Quick tip: If you tell your customer you are going to put them on a brief hold, understand that most customers interpret this to mean 30 seconds or less. If your customer has been on hold longer than that, get back on the phone and reassure them that you are still working to help them.*

- **If you are able, multi-task.** If your customer is on hold and it is taking longer than you anticipated to get the necessary information, use that time to get other important details from your customer. You could say something such as, "My apologies for the delay, Bob. My computer system is slow but, in the meantime, why don't you tell me more about your situation?" This ultimately makes your customer feel heard and reassures them you are using their time wisely.

- **If you can avoid it, do not put a customer on hold while you're working on another customer's issue**. If you're working on resolving a customer's issue, but you have not put your phone in "do not disturb" mode, other customers can call in. You should *never* put a customer on hold while you are resolving another person's issue. This does not respect their time and leads to extended hold times or, worse, leads you to hang up on a new customer if the system does not transfer the call to another representative. If you cannot place your phone in a "do not disturb" mode, be sure to tell your customers that you will follow up with them by the end of day. This way you can finish their tasks when you get around to it and they won't be staying on hold while you deal with other customers.

- **If you aren't going to talk to them, *do* put your customer on hold**. Hearing the clacking of keys and the background chatter of your office can make your customer feel like you are not paying attention to them or their issue. Putting them on hold can be a sign of respect. Even if there is no hold music, silence is better than busy office noise for most people.

- **Consider the influence of hold music, or the lack thereof, on your customer.** According to a study conducted with 30,000 callers by USA Business Telephone Today[3], 52%

of callers put on a silent hold dropped off the line during a 60 second hold period. Only 13% of callers put on a hold with music dropped off the line during that time. The majority of customers on the silent hold who did stay on the line for the one minute estimated that their hold time exceeded 5 minutes. Conversely, the majority of those customers with the music hold determined their hold time to be less than a minute. Consider that hold music can impact your customer's perception of time. Be mindful of this.

Follow-Up Time

If I can impart one piece of advice when it comes to following up with a customer, it's to be as efficient as possible.

Follow these steps to maximize efficiency:

- **Ask yourself: does the customer *need* a follow-up?** It's always best to resolve the issue while the customer is on the phone with you. If you are able, you should always take care of a customer's issue during the initial call. There is a saying that goes, "Lazy people work twice." If you delay work that could be done immediately, you might end up having to do more work when you *do* get to the issue. In addition to the work you would have done before, you'll also have to do the work of recalling details about the original interaction. Consider also that if a follow-up requires you to store sensitive information such as a social security or credit card number, you're putting your customer at risk by delaying the process.

- **Identify whether an email or a call back is the right option for your customer**. Do you need to work through an issue with them on the phone or is it a matter of simply confirming that an issue has been resolved? If it is the latter, an email may suffice. Although it may take longer for you to type out an email than calling a customer back, it will often be quicker for the customer to receive an email than a phone call. If that choice is yours, always choose the option that will save time for the customer, not you..

- **Once you decide on the method of follow-up, make sure that their contact information is correct.** If you are calling a customer back, be sure to repeat the phone number you have on file and confirm it is correct. If you are emailing them with follow-up information, send a test email while they are on the phone.

- **Give the customer a timeline for follow-up.** Tell the customer when they should anticipate an email or follow-up call from you. Five minutes? An hour? End of day? Your customer needs to know. They have other things to do besides wait around to hear back from you.

- **If the follow-up is delayed, apologize.** Sometimes, factors outside your control will prevent you from getting back to a customer on time. When that happens, your first action when you do connect with the customer should be to apologize for the delay.

- **Use that Do Not Disturb function.** If you have the option to address a customer's issue immediately after the interaction, do it. The sooner you get back to a customer, the more respect you show and the more trust you maintain. If you take another call, especially if you told the customer you would get back to them in a short amount of time, you sully that trust. Likewise, if you take a call and immediately put the new customer on hold by telling them you're "wrapping up with another customer," you are letting them know your previous customer's time is more important than theirs. So, if possible, hit that "Do Not Disturb" button. Task management is an important part of respect.

4. WHAT YOUR CUSTOMER SAYS

"One is the loneliest number that you'll ever do." Three Dog Night, One

Every interaction with a customer is two-sided. What your customer says matters and should be treated as such. Part of respect is ensuring that your customer feels that you are listening to them and they are part of the solution.

That's why any conversation with a customer should be *active*. Do your best to elicit responses from your customer so they are reassured you are hearing them and they feel they are working *with* you toward a solution.

Even if their part of working toward a solution is as simple as providing necessary information, actively involving

them in this process will lay a foundation of mutual respect.

5. WITHHOLDING JUDGMENT

"You can't judge an apple by looking at a tree/You can't judge honey by looking at the bee/You can't judge a daughter by looking at the mother/You can't judge a book by looking at the cover"-Bo Diddley, You Can't Judge a Book By It's Cover

In the last chapter, we explored how judgement is the enemy of understanding. It is also the enemy of respect. It is easy in customer service (and life in general) to judge people by the way they speak, act, and dress. Every day we make quick judgments of people in our interactions. In customer service, while it's not always possible to eliminate judgment, we can *reserve* judgment. Part of respect is treating people like the human beings they are. Give *them* the opportunity to tell *you* who they are, instead of assigning them a role. That is not your place.

This brings us back to the platinum rule: Treat others *better* than you want to be treated.

If you apply only the golden rule and assume that a person wants the same things as you it can lead to discord. By applying the platinum rule you give the person the benefit of the doubt and allow them the respect to be seen as a person who is simply looking for help in their own way.

When I was first starting to work customer service at a bank, a customer came in who many people might consider "eccentric." She was in her late 90's, loquacious, and purposefully chose to dress in worn-out, ill-fitting clothes to give the impression that she was homeless. At the time, I didn't realize she was a regular at the bank. She chose to come up to my desk. I gave her the respect of assuming that she was a customer, like everyone else in the bank, and I listened. After about 15 minutes of talking about non-financial topics, she told me she needed assistance with her account. She gave me her account number and I helped her.

After we were through, she looked me right in the eye and said, "You're new here. I know everyone who works here. You didn't even bat an eye at how I look. You treated me like I was human. I try to avoid coming into the bank because everyone else treats me so poorly. It shouldn't be that way, should it?"

No, it shouldn't be that way. Everyone, no matter their station, deserves respect. As a customer service agent, you are in a unique position to give respect to people, some of whom don't get much of it on a daily basis. It is up to you to reserve judgment, even if someone is loud, wears odd clothing, or doesn't have the knowledge you think they should have.

It is your job to be heartbreakingly human to them.

6. OWNING YOUR MISTAKES

"If I could turn back time/If I could find a way/I'd take back those words that've hurt you and you'd stay." -Cher, If I Could Turn Back Time

You won't be perfect. Sometimes factors like technology, co-workers, or conflicting responsibilities interfere with our ability to show the utmost respect to our customers. In those situations, the smartest thing you can do is acknowledge the gaps in your service, take responsibility for your role in those gaps, and honor the customer's experience.

Let's say there are 10 people working in your call center and 15 calls come through around the same time. This is an unusually high call volume for your center. You promise the customer you are talking to that you will follow up with them by email within 10-15 minutes, not knowing there are other customers waiting. As soon as you hang up, another call comes through before you can put your phone on "Do Not Disturb" mode. Since it would be rude to make this customer wait while you take care of another customer, you address their issue...which takes 15 minutes. Right after you hang up with customer #2, you receive a frantic email from customer #1 asking why they haven't received an email yet.

Here's what you should do:

First and foremost, apologize to customer #1 in the first line of your email. Acknowledge that your email was delayed due to an unusually high volume of calls. Now, here's where it gets tricky. When taking responsibility, the best move isn't always to admit fault outright, especially in a case like this where the customer emailed right at the end of the aforementioned deadline. In this case saying "I messed up" can diminish the respect a customer has for you. However, you can still own that the situation caused your customer discomfort. Take the opportunity to acknowledge the customer's experience: "I'm sorry the delay caused you stress." Continue by thanking the customer for their patience, and then proceed with the necessary information. Word to the wise: When honoring the customer's experience, avoid the word "if " (e.g. "I'm sorry *if* the delay caused you stress"). When a customer has told you how they felt, believe them. Using the word "if " implies ambiguity and distrust of their version of events. At the end of the day, the best way to apologize when you have erred is a change in behavior. Do your best to rectify the situation and ensure the customer will not have a repeat experience.

THE CHALLENGES OF RESPECT

"We're not gonna take it/Oh no, we ain't gonna take it/We're not gonna take it anymore." -Twisted Sister, We're Not Gonna Take It

Cultivating respect is difficult. Most of us learned the basic principles of respect at a young age. However, what makes it challenging is that respect can be interpreted differently depending on culture, personality, gender...you name it! What some people view as a sign of respect, others might see as an insult.

To counteract this challenge you can *listen*. Use your foundation of patience and understanding to aid in interpreting how your customer wants to be treated. Be attuned to your customer's verbal, physical, and tonal cues to assess what resonates with them.

One challenge with respect is that sometimes you can be perfect with your intent, your reception of your customer, and your delivery of information, and the customer can still be determined to pick a fight with you. While you might respect your customer, that does not always mean they will respect you. Sometimes, whether another person has respect for you is completely outside of your control. You may fail to maintain respect for the customer in those situations. And that's ok. I've been there.

While I was working at a call center for a national bank, a man called in one evening and immediately started cussing me out. He was angry at me, angry at the bank, and probably angry at life in general. To date, I have never had a customer use more hurtful, foul expletives than this man.

I couldn't take it. I put the man on hold thinking it would give both of us time to cool off before continuing the conversation. Big mistake. The customer cussed me out for putting him on hold. I barely got his name and his bank account number between the swear words. I couldn't get him to tell me anything about the issue he needed help with.

I had hit my limit. Finally, I shouted back defensively, "What do you want from me?" This only fanned the flame. His insults became so egregious that I actually hung up on him.

I was in tears.

Unfortunately, that evening there were only 3 employees working and no managers. So, when the customer called back, I had the misfortune of getting him *again*. The conversation went a little like this,

"Are you the b**ch who hung up on me?"

Deep breath. "Sir, how is it that I can help you today?"
"Well, you can f*ck right off!"

"Sir, f*ck right off is not part of our services, how can I help you?"

"Oh, you think you're SO SMART?"

By this point, a kind co-worker had seen my fat tears, my clenched fists, and the words I was doing my damndest to bite back...

He stepped in. Thank God. He acted as the supervisor and said, "Ok, sir, do you want our help or would you like to end our call at this time?" In part because of my friend's calm ultimatum and in part because of his role as a 'supervisor', the man finally calmed down and they were able to resolve his issue.

I went to the bathroom and wept on the tile floor for 10 minutes all the while thinking, *"People suck. I hate them."*

While there will be days when it *feels* like that, it's not true. People don't suck. Most of them aren't worth hating. Sometimes in customer service, it can seem like the world is made up of terrible people. If it's any comfort, in my experience, these types of people make up less than 1% of all people you will talk to throughout your career.

If you still aren't at ease, here are a few more stats to help convince you the majority of people aren't, at their core, jerks:

- A 2018 Stanford study found that 74% of all conflicts on Reddit are caused by 1% of users[4]
- A 2013 study found that 63% of all violent crimes in Sweden committed over a span of three decades was committed by 1% of people.[5]
- A 2013 BMJ Quality & Survey study found that 3% of all Australian doctors were responsible for 49% of all complaints.[6]

Translation: The minority causes the majority of problems.

It's a reliable enough phenomenon to rest easy on the assumption that the next customer on your line will, in all likelihood, be one of the good ones. And, if they *are* one of the troublemakers, they are one of the few.

So, let's address *why* some people have trouble respecting you.

It boils down to a few reasons:

#1: They're not in your head

In the last chapter we discussed that people often overestimate how effective we are at getting across the point we are trying to make. Just as you are not in your customers' heads, they are not in yours. The difference is that your customers are usually not working toward seeing the world from your perspective. This can lead to misunderstanding.

You would think after the 70+ years call centers have existed, people would be familiar with the customer service process. This is simply not true. People will make the mistake, particularly if you work for a large company, of assuming you are *one in a thousand* representatives working that day...so why should they have to wait? Do you really have other callers waiting? Does it really take your computer that long to load? Why isn't the refund credit processing faster? You and I know that, when it comes to call centers, you are lucky to be *one in a hundred* representatives. And sometimes technology runs a little slow. And credits do take a few days to process. But the customer doesn't know that.

#2: They are having a bad day

Bad days happen to us all. Your customer wants someone to blame. They want someone to take it out on. Congratulations, that person is you.

#3: They are, unfortunately, biased against you

As we all know, prejudice exists. Sometimes the simple fact that you are *you* makes a customer inclined to discriminate against you. It's not fair and it's not right, but it happens.

#4: They're pranksters

Kids love prank calls. It's annoying. It's disrespectful. But it happens...particularly if you work at a 24-hour call center. My advice? Remember you were 13 once too.

While in interpersonal relationships you may have the freedom to require respect from your loved ones, the same is not true in a customer service interaction. Even if a customer isn't being respectful toward you, you must always be respectful toward them. However, that doesn't mean you cannot set boundaries in situations where a customer is being blatantly disrespectful. No one should take advantage of your kindness.

Here are a few boundary setting tips:

#1: Mirror pace, not attitude

When someone is unreasonable, it might be tempting to give them a taste of their own medicine. However, when you do this, you risk reflecting disrespect back onto them, especially if they are using foul language.

#2: Check-and-redirect

Let's say a customer yells at you as you pick up the phone, "Were you aware I was on hold for 20 minutes?" In this scenario, imagine that callers are sent to the first available operator, so you are unaware of your caller's hold time before you pick up the phone. You can give a small check to the customer to clarify the situation. Then, you can offer them an opportunity to redirect the conversation. A successful check-and-redirect might go something like this, "I was not aware you were on hold for 20 minutes. We do have a high volume of calls at this time. Now that you're with me, and I do understand that you are on a time crunch, let's see what we can do to get your questions answered as soon as possible so you can go about your day."

#3: Remind them you are on their side and tell them how they can help you help them

If your customer is intent on belligerence, a good way to redirect them is to remind them that *you* are there to help *them*. This is

especially useful if they are swearing. Try something like this, "Mr. Smith, I am here to help you. The best way for me to help you is for you to bear with me and refrain from using foul language. That will help this situation go quickly and efficiently."

#4: Give them an option to leave the conversation

This is the technique my co-worker used with the unreasonable bank customer at the beginning of this section. He told the customer he could end the conversation or receive our help. Those were the two options. Likewise, if you are being consistently rebuffed by your customer when you are trying to get answers, you can offer them the option to end the conversation. But you should only do this if the customer is refusing to comply. That process might look something like this:

"Mrs. Jones, I understand you are frustrated. I am here to help you. I need to ask you some questions in order to get details of your situation which will allow me to assist you. Is that something you want to do at this point in time?"

If they are still antagonistic, you can respond with,

"Based on your response, it seems you're not prepared to do that. If you'd like to file a complaint, we can do that or you can give us a call back when you're ready to take action to resolve the issue. Which would you like to do?"

By asking questions and giving them options, you are still showing them respect because you are letting them decide whether they want help or not.

#5: Lean on co-workers for assistance

My kind co-worker at the bank saved me from a very difficult customer. If a customer is unmanageable, you can speak to a manager or supervisor. If neither one is around, look for an experienced co-worker. Likewise, if you see your co-worker struggling with a difficult customer and you have the ability and experience, offer your help. Remember, they are on your team.

#6: In the case of prank calls, I give you permission to hang up

You do not need to indulge pranksters. Just hang up and go about your day.

#7: Try your very best not to take these scenarios personally

If you have done your job and shown up, you are honoring your role as a customer service representative. Whatever your customer puts on you after that is their own shortcoming.

Remember, the beauty of respect is that you are able to show compassion to your customer without internalizing their emotions. When you face a difficult customer, remember this facet of respect. Respect is not martyrdom. Respect gives you a way to show humanity and preserve your own. By embracing this principle, you can come to the conclusion that respect does not only apply to your customer, but to you as well. You are also deserving of respect. If your customer won't give it to you, then it is up to you to give it to yourself.

FOR THE MANAGERS

"Oh, baby I get by with a little help from my friends."-Joe Cocker, With a Little Help From My Friends

As a manager, respect the fact that your representatives are dealing with difficult customers *every single day*. Anything you can provide to lighten this burden will help your employees maintain respect for your customers.

Here are a few words of wisdom to help you create the right environment for respect in your workplace:

#1 Run sample scenarios with potential employees.

When it comes to elements of respect such as tone, pace, and conflict management, it's important to observe how you and others interpret a potential employee's intent. Sometimes the best way to do that is to run sample scenarios to see how they react in the moment. Even though someone could *know* the right steps to take, they could instinctually react in a disrespectful way. This is a quick way to assess whether they can represent your company in high pressure situations.

After you hire someone, monitor them closely over a 90 day period to ensure they have enough resiliency to withstand the daily dose of challenging customer interactions.

#2 Create an online form for complaints.

In order to preserve your employee's ability to have compassion for other members of the human race, it might be beneficial to give customers a way to voice their grievances through a third-party medium. This way, your employees do not need to be burdened by complaints. Create an online form that customers can find through a simple internet search, or that a representative can refer a hostile customer to. This allows impartial AI to appease the armchair critics and preserve your customer service rep's sanity.

#3 Check in with your employees.

There is only so much negativity and anger that one person can take. Even if your employee has naturally thick skin, the job can be overwhelming. It's important to check in periodically with your employees to make sure they have the tools to withstand this stress. Show respect to your employees by reassuring them that they have a trustworthy support system when they are dealing with difficult clients.

#4 Offer a callback service for customers on hold.

Many call centers with a high volume of calls have implemented an automatic callback service. This gives an approximate time range when the customer will be called back and ensures that the customer will not need to be on hold for an hour waiting to be served. This way, when the customer does finally talk to one of your employees, they will not be angry they had to listen to "Careless Whisper" five times.

#5 Choose your hold music wisely.

A 2014 Study in the Journal of Applied Psychology[7] found pop music with neutral lyrics was generally the best received by customers. (One more reason for my earworm song choices in this chapter).

Consider also including a message with your hold music. Remember the USA Business Telephone Today survey we mentioned before? While 50% of customers dropped the call with no music and 13% of customers dropped the call with music, only 2% of customers dropped the call with music *and* a message to the customer.

As we've seen, patience begets understanding. Understanding and patience lay the groundwork for respect. All three of these qualities create an attitude of service which builds an environment that is well-suited for a positive customer experience. In the next section, we'll explore *how* these qualities blend into the perfect customer service experience.

PILLAR FOUR:

EXPERIENCE

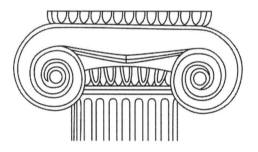

PILLAR FOUR: EXPERIENCE

Bringing It All Together To Find A Solution

"Our first impressions are generated by our experiences and our environment, which means that we can change our first impressions . . . by changing the experiences that comprise those impressions."

— *MALCOLM GLADWELL*

I couldn't have said it better myself, Mr. Gladwell.

Create the right experience and you'll create the right first impression.

How do you create the right experience?

To start, you need the proper foundation. The proper foundation is the attitude of service that you have built through developing your patience, understanding, and respect.

Think of it like making a chocolate cake:

Patience is the flour
Understanding is the sugar
Respect is the chocolate
Experience is the grand icing on the cake.

You must blend all the ingredients—patience, understanding, and respect—together *before* you add on the experience. Then? You are ready to serve.

Malcolm Gladwell also wrote a wonderful book called *Outliers*, in which he examined what made high-achieving people stand out from the crowd. Were they exceptionally lucky? Were they simply born under the right star? Were they predestined, once-in-a-generation type people?

No. Becoming a high-achieving person had less to do with an individual's inherent skills and more to do with factors such as their culture, generation, and formative experiences. The same, I believe, is true of businesses. High-achieving businesses are not just lucky, they are successful because they have the right foundation, and because of the experiences they provide. The good news is that you have control over that foundation and those experiences.

Following in Malcolm Gladwell's footsteps, I wanted to know: who were the "outlying" businesses in terms of customer service experience?

In 2018, Forbes put together a list of the top 20 U.S. businesses ranked with the highest overall customer service satisfaction according to the American Customer Satisfaction Index (ACSI)[1]. Since our goal is to examine what makes a good customer service experience, we'll explore this chapter with testimonials straight from customers of some of those top 20 companies.

Let's start with this customer review from ACSI top-rated company Trader Joes:

"From the selection of products that you can only get there to the quality of service you can get nowhere else, they're always my first choice. Trader Joe's products are the standard by which I measure other stores."

The goal with experience is to leave the customer feeling like you are the golden standard by which they judge all other companies.

An example of this phenomenon in action:

Remember when I told you about my experience with the first touchscreen ATMs? My colleagues and I learned everything we could about the new touchscreen ATMs, right down to the tone of each button. While I told you that customers were impressed with our intimate knowledge of the new technology, what I didn't tell you was how this *directly* impacted the business. A few months after we started working customer service on the ATMs, we were informed that the number of newly opened bank accounts had *skyrocketed* in the previous quarter.

At first, the bank thought this was a simple seasonal spike but when we asked the new clients, "What made you decide to open up an account with our bank?" the majority responded enthusiastically with, "The ATMs!" It turns out these new clients were so impressed with the quality and enthusiasm of service at the new ATMs, that they decided to open accounts. If they could trust the ATMs, they could trust the bank. Not only that, but these customers then referred our bank to their friends and family. By being at the forefront of this technological revolution and setting the standard for good customer service at ATMs, we increased our client base and customer loyalty. This experience ingrained in me a valuable lesson:

A company's reputation can be made by its customer service.

Just as you can gain business by creating a forward-thinking, customer-first environment, you can *lose* business if you fail to do so. If you rely solely on your products and sales to retain customers, you run the risk of losing clientele when your services falter. Every business has failures. What makes the difference when it comes to customer retention is a good customer service experience.

Take Dell, for instance. In the late 1990's, Dell had some of the best computers on the market. Their sales were flourishing. And then...the technology changed. There were malfunctions with the newer models, their computers were susceptible to viruses, and their customers became irate. This may have been an easy hurdle to overcome if Dell wasn't also notorious for poor customer service at the time. When customers would call in, Dell service representatives ran them through *every possible* way to repair the computer before concluding, "Well, it is what it is," and leaving their hapless customers stranded with their broken computers. Customers blasted Dell for their terrible service and Dell experienced a substantial dip in sales. They were soon outperformed by companies such as HP and Compaq.

If Dell had prioritized the customer experience during that time by opting to limit the number of hoops a customer had to go through during a call, shipping computer replacements free of charge, and approaching their customers with compassion, they may not have suffered the substantial loss in clientele.

Many companies mistakenly believe that taking extra steps to satisfy customers will be costly. But the goal is to make the customer a **lifelong customer**. If you provide the right service, your customers will buy from you again. If you do it right, they also will spread the word about your company to their friends and family. In the end, customer retention is more valuable than any singular product or experience. Yes, you may see a temporary loss in profit, but the reputation earned will be worth every penny paid.

Dell learned their lesson. In my office today, Dell is the only computer brand we use. This is not because they are the only good computer on the market, but because they took the feedback about their customers' dissatisfaction and course-corrected. They put an onus on improving the customer service experience. Now, when we have an issue with our computers, Dell will send someone out to our offices by the next day *at the latest*. A fairy tale ending if I've ever heard one.

As a customer service representative *and* as a business, your goal should be to create an experience that is a win-win for you and your customers. If your customers feel satisfied, their loyalty will help your business grow.

THE SECRET INGREDIENTS OF A GOOD EXPERIENCE

Patience, understanding, and respect aren't enough for a good experience because these qualities alone can't guarantee results. While the first three pillars can set the stage for a potentially good interaction, subtle nuances can boost or blunder a customer's experience.

An Important Memo To All the Managers, Trainers, and CEOs: While a representative could have done everything in their power to create a good experience for their customer, if your business hasn't fostered the right environment then their efforts may be fruitless. A good customer experience grows out of a company's foundation. With this in mind, I will first address the secrets of a good experience for customer service representatives, and then for businesses at large.

HOW TO CREATE A GOOD CUSTOMER SERVICE EXPERIENCE AS A REPRESENTATIVE

As I said in the Introduction, your most important role as a customer service representative is to be an **advocate** for your customer. That means that your primary concern should be getting a customer what *they* want, how they want it. It should be your prerogative to make them feel good. With that in mind, let's talk about a few ways that you can create a feel-good, customer-first experience.

GET RESULTS

"They always have the most accurate results."

— *CUSTOMER ABOUT GOOGLE*

A customer's #1 desire is results. Without results, the customer's experience deteriorates. You may have patience, understanding, and respect in spades, but without a concrete positive outcome these qualities may not hold much water.

I cannot tell you *how* to get results for your specific industry. However, I can say that there are ways to *deliver* results that can create a good experience for your customer:

#1: Give only the details your customer wants

Sometimes, your customer will only want a simple confirmation that their result has been achieved. "Mr. Mack, we've applied credit and it'll show up in your account in 10 days. Do you have any questions?" Sometimes, however, a customer will want a lengthier explanation, "Mr. Mack, we've applied the credit to your account. What will happen next is that our company will contact your bank. Your bank will then hold it to ensure there is no error and they may possibly reach out to you for confirmation. If there is no discrepancy, your bank will apply the credit to your account. This whole process is going to take about 10 business days."

The trick for assessing whether or not a given customer wants a detailed explanation of the process is simple: Ask them.

#2: Do not end the interaction before you are certain it is resolved

Take the time to lead the customer where they need to go and don't let up until you're 100% sure they're either at their destination or will reach their destination. Inevitably, a few customers will grow impatient with this process. For those customers, one of my favorite sayings is, "I want to make sure we get you to a cruising altitude and then I'm out of your way." This conveys that you are concerned about their results and are taking the time because you want to ensure they will not re-encounter the issue.

#3: Explain it in a way they understand

This goes back to the use of jargon that we've discussed in previous chapters. Make your language accessible so the customer not only gets the results they want, but also understands those results.

#4: Do a double-check to ensure they got what they needed

At the end of delivering results, double-check with your customers to make sure they don't have any lingering questions. "Have we solved everything? Would you like any further assistance?"

BE FRIENDLY

"The people that work there. They make shopping a pleasure!"

— *CUSTOMERS ABOUT PUBLIX*

For an overall good experience, there is one quality beyond results and beyond an attitude of service that can drastically alter a customer's perception of your company: Friendliness.

In fact, one study [2]examining customer-employee relationships in 169 retail stores showed that friendliness not only directly impacted a customer's perception of service experience in the store, but it affected a customer's willingness to return to a store and spread positive reviews about the business to their friends post-experience.

Friendliness, of course, cannot replace getting results. It can, however, amplify good experiences and help to mitigate bad ones.

. . .

BE QUICK

"Wow! 25 cars deep in the drive-thru and we got our food in less than 7 minutes. Who does that? Chick-Fil-A of course! They know how do do it."

— *CUSTOMER AT CHICK-FIL-A*

Time is precious. The quicker you can get from problem to result, the more grateful your customer will be.

Take the time to train yourself to be efficient with your customer's time. Hopefully you have a script that gives you the basic tools to make this possible, but I also encourage a bit of trial-and-error to see how you can quickly achieve results *and* maintain the proper attitude of service.

FOLLOW-UP

Once results are achieved, the interaction is not complete. Follow up with your customer. Ensure that there haven't been any subsequent issues and ask for their feedback. As a bonus, you not only give your customer an opportunity to share their opinions and concerns, but you also might get some great testimonials for your business during the follow-up.

Want to go the extra mile? When a product or service you offer changes, reach out to regular customers to give them advance notice of impending changes and ask whether they have any questions. Once the changes have been implemented, follow up with your regulars to ensure they understand the features and ask whether they'd like any assistance in exploring the new dynamics.

ACKNOWLEDGING THE MILESTONES

Follow-up isn't the only way to make your customer feel seen. Acknowledging milestones for regular customers (birthdays, anniversaries, etc.) makes them feel valued.

If your company deals with regular customers, then hopefully you already have the technology in place to automatically send out these kinds of acknowledgements. However, if this is not a feature, and you are dealing with a manageable number of regular clients, go the extra step to reach out via email to acknowledge these occasions.

MAKE YOUR CUSTOMER FEEL SAFE

When a customer comes to you with an issue, they are often in a moment of vulnerability. They are frustrated and fearful because this problem is impeding their normal flow of daily life. They need you to help them out. In order to create an experience that makes them feel open to working toward a solution, you must first make them feel safe.

I created company, **Authentic Voice LLC**, with another professional Celeste DeCamps. Our business conducts workshops and lectures to coach people in public speaking. It is specifically geared toward people who are preparing for a major speech or presentation. Currently, 31.2% of people in the U.S. are afraid of public speaking[3]. Ipso facto, when people come to our company for help, they are often in a hyper-vulnerable state.

One of the overarching pieces of feedback from our customers at Authentic Voice is that we made them feel safe. That safety enabled them to calm themselves enough to be receptive to learning. How did we make these customers *feel* safe? Beyond using a foundation of patience, understanding, and respect, Celeste and I instilled a perception of safety by being *relatable*. Since we know that most people in this workshop came to us with a fear of public speaking, we asked participants at the start of each workshop to share what brought them there. When they share this fear of public speaking, they feel a sense of comradery and safety. They know other people in the group have the same struggles as they do.

In customer service, you may not have had the same experience as your customer. However, there are less direct ways you can establish relatability. For example:

"I'm so sorry you're going through that. I would be really frustrated by that issue as well."

"I hear you're struggling with your internet connection. I had another customer who also had the same issue this morning. We were able to resolve it quickly using x, y, z. Let's start there."

"Sarah. Oh, that's my sister's name, too. I love that name."

These are simple hacks to draw a direct line between you and your customer. Once you've established that connection, you open up the way for an experience in which your customer feels like they've developed a genuine bond with you.

BE THE ONE STOP SHOP

The staff went out of their way to be certain all my concerns were addressed, scheduled a loaner auto and completed the work as promised and on time. They followed up to assure me there were no outlying problems. I will continue to bring my auto here for service.

— *CUSTOMER ABOUT LEXUS*

Being the "one-stop-shop" for your customer is the ideal scenario. Part of the trouble with customer service these days is that customers tend to feel like they are just another number in the system. Passing a customer along between representatives can make them feel like they are just 'pawned off' to be another person's problem. If you can be that singular point of contact, you will make them feel like you are focused on them.

That said, sometimes you *have* to transfer a customer to another department. In those scenarios, it is crucial that you "take the ball to the end zone." In other words, don't just transfer the customer by sending them over to the other department without explanation. Be upfront about the transfer and stay on the line until the transfer is complete. Here's the four-step process I advise:

1. Be transparent with the customer about why you need to transfer the call and how the other representative will help them resolve their issues. (e.g. "Alright, Samantha, I'm going to need to transfer you to Jennifer in our Sales Department who can help you purchase that limited edition jacket.")

2. Assure the customer that you will stay on the line with them until the transfer is complete. (e.g. "Don't worry, I'll stay on the line with you until Jennifer picks up to ensure the call goes through.")

3. Introduce the customer to the new representative. (e.g. "Samantha, this is Jennifer in our Sales Department. Jennifer, this is Samantha who is looking to purchase the limited edition jacket.")

4. Give the customer a lifeline back to you. (e.g. "It's been a pleasure helping you, Jennifer. If you get disconnected or have any further issues, here is my extension so you can call me back directly. Thank you.")

REMEMBER, YOU ARE POWERFUL

As a customer service agent **you are powerful**. You have incredible influence not only over your customer's experience in the span of one interaction, but over their experience with your company as a whole.

With this power, it becomes even more important to abide by the platinum rule: Treat your customer better than you want to be treated.

Taking that extra step to give your customer what they need is a small gesture that can make a *big* difference. Showing that extra bit of compassion in a difficult moment can win you a customer for life.

Of course, there will always be elements about your customer's experience that are outside your control. Your customer might be on the heels of an angry divorce and out for a fight, there might be a company-wide technological glitch, or your customer could be annoyed by the Taylor Swift song that was playing while they were on hold. Just know that, these incidences aside, what you do is important. In fact, you are *the most important link* between your customer and your business. Remember that, and you'll produce astounding service experiences.

HOW TO CREATE A GOOD CUSTOMER SERVICE EXPERIENCE AS A REPRESENTATIVE

Trainers, managers, and business owners play a substantial role in creating an environment that is welcoming for customers. While a customer service representative can do their best to be an advocate for a single customer, you must accept that it is your responsibility to be an advocate for *all* of your customers.

This means you must aim to create a positive brand experience that is tailored to your clientele as a whole.

Here are a few ways to create that experience:

Find Out Who Your Customer Is and Cater Directly to Them

"Aldi has everything I need at the lowest prices in a small area that feels like a Mom and Pop store. I love the personal feel of the store combined with the high quality and low prices every day."

— *CUSTOMERS ABOUT ALDI*

As a business, it's important to know who your customer is. Part of creating a memorable experience is making sure that experience is customized to *your customer's* likes and dislikes. I recommend building profiles for your existing and ideal customers. Investigate their hobbies, professions, geographical regions, food preferences, preferred wake-up time, etc.

After you do this reconnaissance, ask yourself questions such as, "What is most important to my customer?" "What is my customer looking for in their service experience?" Use the answers to these questions to develop a business experience that is relatable and accommodates the lifestyle of your customer.

Let's compare Apple and Samsung. Apple customers are typically tech-savvy folks who want to get the jump on the latest trend. Apple knows this so they build hype for new products, put a premium on being ahead of the game, and encourage their customers to line up around the block for the newest release. Samsung, on the other hand, caters to people who aren't as concerned about the newest, flashiest thing. Their customers prioritize a product that is reliable, has longevity, and works well. They're not the kind of people who will line up for the first edition of a phone, bugs and all. They'll wait for the 3rd edition when all the kinks have been worked out. Samsung's prices and product consistency reflect this business model, just as Apple's innovation-first attitude reflects theirs.

If you're a small-scale, regional store you can absolutely compete with larger companies in customer service.

Go the extra mile to cater to customers *in your community*. For example, if you own a niche store that specializes in high-end musical equipment you might find yourself losing business to the large, corporate musical store across the road because they can afford to lower their prices. However, that store closes at 6 PM. You know that many of your clients are more active at night, so you choose to keep your business open between 12 PM and 10 PM instead of the typical 8 AM - 6 PM hours. Since you're keeping in line with your custom- er's preferred hours, you will get more business. If you're open at the exact moment when a customer might need a quick repair on a guitar pickup before their 9 PM gig, you'll gain a customer for life. Why? Because your business model was built to accommodate your customer's lifestyle.

For businesses that aren't as niche as Apple, Samsung, or the small-scale music store, the best rule of thumb is to be as available as possible to create the best experience. For example, if you work in industries such as travel or banking, where emergency situations can happen at any time of day, your service line should remain open 24/7 to provide a safety net for your customer. That reliability can ensure your customer never feels stranded. They can count on you to be there for any experience, any time of day.

Gather Testimonials From Each Customer "Type"

Another part of offering a positive experience is getting feedback from your existing customers. The benefits of feedback are two-fold: 1) You get information on how to create a better experience for your customer and 2) You get testimonials to provide third-party reassurance so your potential customers know that people just like them have benefitted from your products and services.

Did you know that at an 86% trust rate, word of mouth is *the most influential marketing tool*[4]?

A few more quick stats that show the power of good testimonials[5]:

1. 92% of customers read online reviews before buying
2. 72% of consumers said positive reviews increase their trust in a company
3. 88% of consumers trust online reviews as much as word of mouth recommendations from people they know

It's important when asking for customer feedback to strike a fine balance between quality and ease. You don't want to solicit glib feedback that will have little value in improving your service or convincing other potential clients to buy. For instance, if you simply ask a customer, "Did you have a good experience?" most will respond "yes" even if it was really only so-so. Though you may get many "yes" answers, you won't know what it is you're doing right, let alone be able to share those qualities with prospective clients. On the other hand, if you try to solicit several essay-long answers, you'll be disrespecting your client's time.

I was recently asked to complete a post-service customer satisfaction survey for my bank. The entire survey was 15 questions *on the phone*. It took me over 5 minutes to complete and, even though I had a positive experience during the service, this time-wasting survey depleted my perception of the company.

At my company, Authentic Voice, we ask questions that are specific, but do not require lengthy answers. For example, we might ask a customer, "Do you feel you will be using the tools and tips learned in this workshop in your next presentation? Please answer on a scale of 1-5, 1 being 'Not at all' and 5 being 'Absolutely'." If the client then answered with a 5, we can use that review to create a testimonial. (e.g. Cynthia says, "I will absolutely be using the tools and tips learned in this workshop in my next presentation.") And *always* be sure to include an 'other' option for those people who want to give the 'War and Peace' version of their experience. Sometimes, that can be the most valuable feedback of all.

It also is a good idea to add an incentive for feedback to ensure it is a win-win for you and your customer. For example, you could offer anyone who completes your survey 5% off their next shopping experience or access to an exclusive video. This way your survey isn't just another "time suck" with no compensation for your customer's generosity.

One more note about testimonials: If possible, get testimonials for every type of customer you have. At Authentic Voice we have everyone from Senior Analysts to Magazine Publishers and anyone in-between who has benefited from our services. People want to hear from their peers because it is likely that their peers will have a similar experience to them. They want to know what they're in for.

Recently, two women, both in middle management, attended one of our Authentic Voice LLC workshops. Since they both were in similar situations, they relied on each other's feedback. During the workshop, one of these women presented and, at the end, the other woman asked, "Are you presenting to your boss or your boss's boss?" Not being in the industry, this was a question Celeste or I would not have thought to ask. By asking this question, this woman was able to enhance and deepen the presenter's experience with our course *because* she was a peer. She understood our service in a way that we could not.

In the same way, your customer, Anna, might find value in your product that you haven't even considered. And Anna's brother Patrick might find the exact same value if he tried it. You can't relay that value to Patrick, but Anna can.

It's the Little Things

As a business, the little things matter. The small touches that make an experience just a little more pleasant can make all the difference to your customers. Here are a few examples of these touches worth considering:

• One management software company not only uses hold music, but also incorporates a periodic message that includes interesting factoids to keep the listener entertained and engaged.

• Some banks not only have a service teller, but a customer service representative on the floor who will talk to customers in line to see if they can assist with getting a project started while they are waiting.

• Zappos will exchange sizes at no cost to you. Not only that, they'll rush ship you the new size.

• REI allows you to return products at any time. Used or unused. 1 week later or 10 years later.

• Some subscription websites will extend trials if you have unused trial days.

• Wegmans, one of Forbes' Top 20 in Customer service, tailors its decorations to make the customer feel happy. Their customers' testimonials support this: *"The brightness and decorations in the store. It is a very welcoming place."*

What can you offer your customer that would enhance their experience? And don't let the upfront costs deter you! Loyalty and referrals will most likely end up paying you back tenfold.

Give Notice for Change

If you're a growing company, you are always changing. One part of offering a good service experience is to be transparent. If you are going to change your existing products or services in any way, you need to let your customers know.

Many people are averse to change. They have a fear of being left behind. This is why it's essential to take the necessary steps to reassure customers you will be there to hold their hands through all the shifts. Leave no doubt in their mind that they will be included in the new direction.

I recommend sending out an automatic email to all customers *three weeks* prior to any change. Then follow up with them a week before the change, the day before the change, and the day of the change to explain all the new features. Finally, a week after the change, send another email to ask if they have any questions or need any assistance. This way, your customer will see they are not only being included in the changes, but that their experience matters.

You will always get those select few customers who are angry at any changes. Some customers will also manage to miss the notifications and complain. Some, in spite of all communications, will call because they want you to go back to the way things were. In my experience, this is not only how these customers react to change in *this* situation, but how they react to change in life in general.

When you receive these calls, your best bet is to simply offer comfort to your customer, "Yes, it's a change, but it's not the type of change where we're leaving you out in the lurch. We're going to guide you every step of the way." Soon enough, these customers will get used to the change and it will be as if it never happened.

Use AI

"Infinite variety on one site without having to search multiple brands and companies online."

- Customers about Amazon (Forbes Top 20 in Customer Service)

One of the wonderful advances of our modern world is that there are so many self-service options. From automatic check-outs at grocery stores to kiosks in airports that allow you to change your flight without the hassle of waiting in line for an airline attendant, customers are more empowered than ever to be their own helpers.

That said, if you decide to use AI in your customer service, don't completely forego the human element. There are a few reasons for this.

#1: Because glitches happen

If it can go wrong, it will go wrong. Having a customer service representative on hand is like having a script supervisor on a movie set. When the actor forgets and yells "LINE" the script supervisor is there with the line to save the day.

#2: Because some people will want to talk directly to another human being

Recently, a radio network that used to use salespeople to sell advertising time switched over to an exclusively online platform for selling ad space. One salesperson responded, "Well, that's great for the large corporations that barely have time to talk on the phone anyway...but what about the mom and pop shops that have been placing ads for the last 30 years? They don't know the technology. They only know how to do business over the phone." While it's tempting to think all of your customers will advance technologically with you, this just isn't true. You will always be ahead of some customers and you must provide a stepping stone to working with a new system. You do that through personal and human interaction.

#3: Because you need to do follow-up

You might have an automatic recording or text message that customers receive when they try to get in touch with you. You can absolutely use these systems to set up appointments and give customers an easy way to ask questions or voice concerns. Just be sure a real person follows up *quickly,* so they know there is still a human behind the machine.

Have Realistic Expectations for Your Staff

It is critical that you establish realistic expectations for your staff, particularly when it comes to time management.

For example, if you have a busy, detail-oriented call center you can't also expect your customer service representatives to have an average talk time of 1 minute; that is incompatible. It will place unnecessary stress on your representative and reduce the quality of their service. Consequently, the customer's experience will deteriorate. Adjust your expectations for talk time and your staff will offer better service, which is worth more than the time saved.

If you find that after this shift in time expectations, your team cannot cover the volume of calls coming in, then the resolution is simple: **hire more people**. Having the right number of representatives is key enabling your staff to respond to the customer's needs. If you have 1,000 customers and only 5 representatives, you are failing.

A company which I provided consultation, realized the error of having too few representatives on staff. The company handled 1,500 customers and had only 2 customer service representatives. Since they usually received a low volume of customer service calls, 2 representatives seemed enough. However, when there was a software-platform update. The company mistakenly assumed the update would be an easy adjustment for our customers.

Oh, were we wrong.

Even if the changes seem intuitive, remember that it is far better to underestimate your clients than to overestimate them. The office was flooded with frantic customers who did not understand the changes, and the two poor service representatives were drowning in phone calls and emails. Lesson learned.

In this scenario, there were two ways we could have resolved the issue: 1) Hire more staff or 2) If the funds weren't available for additional staffing, do a gradual roll out of the new update so the customer service reps could handle the additional calls.

If you end up with too many cooks in the kitchen you can always opt for temporary employees or re-allocate new customer service reps. There is always more work to be done somewhere.

Choose the Right People

"Dave, Jen and Sean went above and beyond to solve my issue. Their customer service skills set an example of how a customer should be treated. My laptop had 3 previous issues and they replaced it with a new one. That's why Apple is the best!"

-Customer at Apple

Speaking of employees, in order to provide the best customer experience, you must choose the *right* people to be your customer service representatives. As I've expressed before, customer service is not a "filler" job. Customer Service Representatives are the face of your company. The position requires people who are tough-skinned, yet malleable. They should be able to handle difficult customers, adjust to company-wide changes, and work to incorporate customer feedback into their delivery of the customer experience. This takes a special type of person. You can find some tips on how to hire the right representatives in the Conclusion section.

Empower Reps with the Right Tools

As I stated in the previous section, customer service representatives are *powerful*. They can make or break your business. As their supervisor, it is your responsibility to give them the proper tools so they *can* give your customers that gold-star experience. A prepared representative equals a happy customer. Here are a few ways you can empower your representatives:

#1: Teach Your Staff Time Management

As a manager, trainer, or business owner, the onus is on you to give your staff the proper tools to manage their time efficiently. Give them a complete step-by-step guide for quickly moving through a call, and train them with real-world examples until they become comfortable with this flow. This is particularly important for representatives who must deliver detail-oriented responses. Even specifying when during the call to record details, when to ask for a name, when to email a customer, etc. will help prevent your staff from being overwhelmed by a complex process.

FedEx is always on time. My packages arrive safely without any type of damage. They are cautious when placing packages close to my door, yet not out for all to see. They have awesome tracking all along the way.

-Customer about FedEx

#2: Make your staff the one-stop shop

Give your staff the authority to help your customers without needing to go through a third party. For instance, if your company provides financial services, give reps the power to move money around. This will come in handy when a customer calls in who is stuck at a gas station with a car running near empty and a debit card that won't accept the transaction because the restaurant they stopped at for lunch accidentally charged them 5 times, causing an overdraw on their account. If your representative is not authorized to apply instant credit, they will have to go through a supervisor. If one isn't available, your customer will be frustrated *to say the least*, stuck twiddling their thumbs at a gas station in the middle of nowhere. In this scenario, if the representative had authority to apply instant credit, the customer could have quickly been on their way and your company could have followed up with a quality assurance check.

Granting authority to reps gives them the ability to better serve customers in the moment and maintain their position as the customer's singular point of assistance. In the long run, this leads to faster service, less customer frustration, and higher overall customer satisfaction.

#3: Use the P.U.R.E. System

By now, hopefully I've convinced you of the usefulness of this method for both you and your service representatives. Share this system with your employees and use it as a guide toward exceptional service.

#4: Give your staff the right script

A good script is essential. It will be the baseline for all customer interactions. It should be a detailed, thorough, and reliable product knowledge guide for your representatives. A good script will help your reps construct an efficient procedure for each call. It will also need constant revising as your business evolves and as you receive more customer feedback. It should, in no way, be something that is slapped together half-heartedly in a few days.

Writing a good script is one of the most difficult parts of customer service. My company, Authentic Voice, now offers a service where we can work with your company to develop a comprehensive script and standard operating procedures for your customer service representatives. We even offer one-on-one training for you and your staff so that you can "get to cruising altitude" with your customers.

Along with the P.U.R.E. System, Authentic Voice's service will provide you and your representatives with the right tools to become an empowered team that can set the customer service standard for your industry.

"A few months out from training, both the employee and the firm continue to reap the benefits from his private coaching."

-Lindsay Emery (TCC Group) about Authentic Voice LLC

To learn more, email us at pure@authenticvoicellc.com.

THE BOTTOM LINE

With the tools of the P.U.R.E. System—Patience, Understanding, Respect, and Experience—you are now equipped to start developing your customer service strategy.

In the end, it's all about making the customer feel valued.

Remember: Perfect does not exist. It never did. There will always be variables outside of your control that affect how people see your business. However, you are in control of how you see your customer, how you treat your customer, and how you make your customer a priority. With this approach, throughout all the ups and downs of your business, your customer will always know they can depend on one thing: You.

"They actually care about the customer's needs."-Customers about Thrivent Financial

CONCLUSION:

THE P.U.R.E SYSTEM

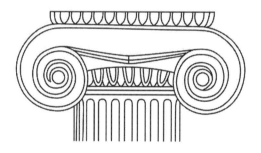

CONCLUSION: THE P.U.R.E. SYSTEM

There you have it! The P.U.R.E. System

Picture your brain forming new connections as you meet the challenge and learn. Keep on going.

— *CAROL DWECK*

This book is about more than customer service. **It is a manual for a mindset.**

I cannot guarantee that by following these steps you will have a smoothly-paved yellow brick road to success, but I can guarantee that you will have a start.

DEAR REPRESENTATIVES,

With the P.U.R.E. System, you can foster genuine person-to-person connections in which you take care of your customer and your business, without sacrificing yourself.

Even if you use the four pillars perfectly, there will be times where your customer kicks you around and you feel like you can't do anything right. After tough interactions like this, it's important to prioritize some self-care. Say to yourself, "Hey, I just had a really hard call. I need to take 3 minutes to reset." Maybe that 3-minute break is a breathing exercise, or a quick walk, or playtime with a Rubix cube. Use any activity that will make you feel cared for in that difficult moment.

In a high-paced call center, this kind of self-care can get lost. We forget that, as reps, we're human too. We can give so much attention to others that we neglect ourselves. In many ways, customer service reps are like punching bags who get repeatedly beat up by angry customers. But even in the gym, after you finish using a punching bag, you need a moment to wipe off all the sweat before the next person can use it. You have to give yourself that moment, too.

If you push yourself to continue working while still fuming from a difficult call, you'll bring that energy with you to your next interaction. This will harm you and your next customer. Take a moment to flush that frustration down the toilet before you pick up the phone again. That way, when you come to the next call, you will be ready to be present in the moment.

Over time, you will start to recover faster from these setbacks. It will get easier. Those bad calls and rough days won't feel so hard because you're taking better care of yourself and growing in resilience. Even the most curmudgeonly customers will be able to recognize your good intent. If they refuse to show up as a kind and capable person, you did. You know that and they know that (even if they'll never admit it!). That's what matters.

Having been a representative *and* a manager *and* a trainer *and* a CEO, let me say this: **I see you.** I appreciate you. If you're doing your best to follow the P.U.R.E. guidelines, then you're doing well in my book. Even if you get knocked around and those difficult customers never seem to see the light, take pride in knowing you work hard to represent your business in a positive light, be of service, and treat your customers like human beings.

I remember the first bank I worked at hearing other customer service reps complaining about customers who would call in to inquire about their balance. "Why are they calling us to ask about their balance when they can get that information themselves?" The thought crossed my mind, *"Well, maybe you're the only person they get to talk to today. We're here for them, if that's what they need. We can't gripe about that. It's what we do."*

It might sound dramatic, but a good customer service representative can change people's lives. There is no one else in the entire company who has their finger on the pulse of the customer the way we do. Maybe you're thinking, *"Yeah, right! Will I really make that much of a difference in someone's day?"* Yes, you will. You will also make a difference for yourself.

I can prove it to you with three of my experiences:

When I was working in IT customer service...

A woman called in a panic because she couldn't figure out how to use GoToMeeting. She had to give an important virtual presentation the next day. When she called, I was already stressed out because a coworker had called in sick, I had reports piling up on my desk, *and* I was supposed to be filling in on the help desk that evening. I knew this lady was going to require a lot of attention. But I took a deep breath, exercised my patience, and embraced my attitude of service. I reminded myself that helping her *was* the most important thing because I work in customer service.

Together, she and I walked through a GoToMeeting tutorial and resolved an issue with her webcam that was interfering with the software. The process took an hour and a half, but by the time we finished, she let out a huge sigh of relief. The next day, she emailed me after the meeting to let me know it went off without a hitch. When I received that message, I knew I made the right decision for her and for myself.

I once worked at a sporting goods retail headquarters in Florida during a merger...

Another team traveled from their headquarters in Colorado to visit our customer service center and assess our operations. The word around the company was that only senior-level employees in our Florida headquarters would be vetted to get transfers to Colorado. Everyone else in our Florida base would lose their jobs during the acquisition.

After a couple of weeks, I received a call from one of the supervisors in the IT department. He recruited me for a position in Colorado and a full transfer!

At the time, I wasn't even in a management position. "Why are you giving this to me?" I asked. "I thought you guys weren't giving positions to anybody."

"We weren't," he said. "But I was asking around about you. People said you know your stuff. They said you're tough without being rude and you get the job done."

All because of great feedback from customers and coworkers, my new headquarters paid for my move to Colorado and set me up in a shiny new apartment. I had made it a point to be the nicest tech in the room and it opened a door for me that I never thought possible. In fact, a few of the names he mentioned of people who recommended me were people who were flat-out mean to me on multiple occasions. I thought they hated me. You never know. Even people who are telling you to your face that you're doing a terrible job might be the ones who say the nicest things behind your back.

When I was leading the Manhattan Toastmasters Club...

There was one incident that demonstrated how much my customer service mindset had spilled over into each facet of my life. I'd had a difficult day at work, I was worn out, and ready to go home. Suddenly, a lady pulled me aside and said she didn't feel ready to give her speech that night. She wanted to cancel so she could have more time to prepare. At first, I wanted to say yes. It would be one less presentation to deal with and I could end the meeting early and get home sooner. But I knew better. I knew her goal was to overcome her fear of public speaking, and she'd been putting off her speech for weeks. As much as I wanted to get home, I wanted to take care of this woman too.

"You've already written the speech," I told her. "Fortunately, during this meeting, your life isn't depending on it. You might as well do the speech now so you can get that practice in. We're all here to support you and make sure you do well."

She did it and she did a great job. The group lauded her with encouraging, positive feedback. At the end-of-year celebration, she spoke about how much Toastmasters had helped her. "There was one night when I was about to quit," she said. "I was ready to leave Toastmasters for good. I told Michele I didn't want to do my speech, but she convinced me to go ahead. That moment changed everything."

DEAR MANAGER, TRAINER, AND CEO,

Using the P.U.R.E. System will give your customers a patient, understanding, respectful, and results-oriented experience. Better experiences make for better customers. Implementing these guidelines will help solidify your customer base and grow your business. And those aren't the only benefits of this system. As you train your customer service representatives on how to care for other people, this mindset will spill over to their everyday lives. This will create happier, healthier people who are intent on bringing good to this world. Happier employees mean a better business. To help your business embrace the P.U.R.E. philosophy, I propose two addendums to your existing business mission and vision. These will serve as guideposts when you and your team make customer service decisions.

P.U.R.E. Mission: Elevate customer service to a place where individuals approach each other with a level of respect and kindness, which opens doors for conversations where thoughts and ideas are heard.

P.U.R.E. Vision: Impact lives by cultivating opportunities for authentic communication, self-expression, and connection that results in a win-win for everyone involved.

Customer service in which there is a high level of respect, kindness, and results, should be the *norm*. It shouldn't be an exception. People shouldn't expect customer service reps to be rude. Customers should always be able to assume they are going to receive exceptional service anywhere they go.

As an industry, we need to course-correct. Let's make kindness the standard. We need to welcome people in and assure them that when they talk, we will listen.

Even with the bad apples, remember that having customers reach out to your business is a good thing. Those interactions let you know what your company is and isn't doing right. Feedback from your customers should be accepted and encouraged. It gives you the opportunity to retool your product and services.

As a business, I challenge you to set the standard in your field for customer service. It is up to you to be the trailblazer for this revolution.

It starts with you.

Part of your responsibility in this leadership position is to make sure you hire the right people as your customer service representatives. One aspect of the devolution in customer service is the trending belief that customer service is considered a "filler job." It is not a filler job. It requires people to be of a certain disposition. Get the wrong people, and you waste time, lose money and hurt your company's reputation.

Here are qualities you should look for when hiring new service representatives:

QUALITY #1: Malleable

Reps should be able to take instruction and work under pressure in an ever-changing business. If something breaks, you want someone who is committed to finding out how to fix it.

QUALITY #2: Works well under pressure

Some customers will be tough, and some days will be tougher. Your business needs someone who can handle the daily strain. They should be able to answer technical questions and resolve complaints from bullish clients with a calm demeanor.

QUALITY #3: Kind

Employees should inherently know how to be kind. The technical aspects of the job can all be trained, but kindness can't. You need to find people who show a willingness to put themselves into other people's shoes.

QUALITY #4: Self-sufficiency

Being a customer service representative is different from being a receptionist. It's not about transferring the customer to someone else who can help them. Reps need to be able to understand customers' problems without relying on their supervisor.

QUALITY #5: Well-spoken

It is important for your reps to be able to clearly articulate their point both verbally and in writing.

QUALITY #6: A team player

Look for people who recognize they are part of a team. Avoid reps who try to slough off responsibilities with phrases like "That's not my job" or "It's not my fault that happened." When you're interviewing people, give specific examples and ask how the individual would handle it. Ask what they would do with a customer who is exasperated and taking their frustrations out on the rep. Do a little role play and throw phrases at the candidate like, "I need this fixed right away," "You guys messed up," and "What are you going to do about this?" Listen to their response and look for the words "they," "you guys," "those people," and "that department." These words are red flags. Instead, you want to hear words like "I," "me," "my," "us," and "we." If the candidate talks in terms of other people, it's a way of deflecting.

In these test scenarios, be wary of candidates who are inconsistent. A potential representative can start off with empathy and then snap quickly into blame-shifting mode. For instance, "Oh, I'm so sorry you're dealing with that. It looks like *they* messed up your order," or "I'll get this fixed right away. It seems like *the installation team* made a mistake with your setup." Instead of, "I'm so sorry, *we* are going to do everything we can to get this taken care of for you," or "*Our team* will be able to get this sorted out right away."

QUALITY #7: The ability to live up to their words

My brother has a property management company. He has a difficult time hiring because, well, people know how to put on a show. The candidates say they can "repair this" or "paint that" or "I know how to deal with clients"...but then the day comes and they have no idea what they are doing. I tell him, "Give them a test and see how they do. If they say they can repair a leaky pipe, give them a leaky pipe to fix in the super's apartment. Or paint a room. Or use another employee to call in as a customer and see how they handle it." Don't trust words, trust actions.

P.U.R.E. Goes Beyond Customer Service

While it is critical that you choose the right customer service representatives, the P.U.R.E. System is not solely applicable to reps. Even people in sales need to master these skills of serving customers. When salespeople focus on what they can give instead of what they can get, the business will make more sales.

Salespeople are often the customer's first point of contact, so many customers reach out to them with issues. Usually, the sales department will pass customers off to the service team, believing it isn't their job to help with technical issues. However, if the customer feels like they were abruptly disregarded, it can change how they perceive the company as a whole. When it comes time to buy a new product or renew their subscription, they might switch to a provider who makes them feel like a priority.

Salespeople don't need to solve the customer's problem single-handedly, but the customer should be transferred gradually. Look for salespeople who use the *"We"* language. "I can help you and I'm glad you reached out to me. I might bring in someone from the customer support team so we can better assist you."

When hiring *any* position on your team, look for people who embody the *"We"* mentality. If you already have people on your team with a "they" mentality, you are facing an uphill battle, but not all hope is lost. My talented colleague Celeste DeCamps and I currently have a training available to get business teams into a *"We"* mindset. You can learn more about our services at www.authenticvoicellc.com.

A FINAL WORD

Whether you're a representative, a CEO, or a manager, you should be proud to be in the business of serving customers. You have a chance to significantly influence someone's life. Some people feel alone. Others feel abandoned and assume you're going to abandon them too. Some feel like you won't care about what they think or feel. There are even people who don't have family and their only interaction all day is with you. We are their social outlets. We are their teachers, their saviors, and their sounding boards. In some cases, our listening ear can be like therapy to a customer.

It is our privilege to show these people that there is someone in the world who cares about them.

My dream is that customer service once again becomes the place where people are treated with the basic level of empathy and respect that we should all get. We are the people who help to make the world a little more caring, and a little more kind. That's why I'm proud to be in customer service. And I hope you are too.

I slept and dreamt that life was joy. I awoke and saw that life was service. I acted and behold, service was joy.

— *TAGORE*

NOTES

PILLAR ONE: PATIENCE

1. The Official Star Wars Website." StarWars.com. https://www. starwars.com/.
2. *Schnitker, Sarah. (2012). An examination of patience and well-being. The Journal of Positive Psychology. 7. 263-280. 10.1080/17439760.2012.697185.*
3. Diana Kaemingk // October 30. "20 Online Review Stats to Know in 2021." Qualtrics, October 30, 2020. https://www. qualtrics.com/blog/online-review-stats/
4. "TORK SURVEY REVEALS LUNCH BREAK IMPACT ON WORKPLACE ENGAGEMENT." Tork Survey Reveals Lunch Break Impact on Workplace Engagement | Tork US. https://www. torkusa.com/about/pressroom/tbtlb. https://cdntorkprod.blob. core.windows.net/docs-c5/763/185763/original/tork-takes-back-survey.pdf

PILLAR TWO: UNDERSTANDING

1. Santos, Henri C., Michael E. W. Varnum, and Igor Grossmann. "Global Increases in Individualism." Psychological Science 28, no. 9 (September 2017): 1228–39. https://doi.org/10. 1177/0956797617700622.
2. Konrath, Sara H., Edward H. O'Brien, and Courtney Hsing. "Changes in Dispositional Empathy in American College Students Over Time: A Meta-Analysis." Personality and Social Psychology Review 15, no. 2 (May 2011): 180–98. https:// doi.org/10.1177/1088868310377395.
3. L. Newton, "Overconfidence in the Communication of Intent: Heard and Un- heard Melodies," Ph.D. dissertation, (Stanford University, 1990).
4. Ruiz, Miguel, and Janet Mills. 1997. The four agreements: a practical guide to personal freedom.

PILLAR THREE: RESPECT

1. Cohen, D., Nisbett, R. E., Bowdle, B. F., & Schwarz, N., "Insult, aggression, and the southern culture of honor: An "experimental ethnography." 70(5) *Journal of Personality and Social Psychology* 945-960 (1996)
2. Mehrabian, Albert (1971). *Silent Messages* (1st ed.)
3. USA Business Telephone Today Survey (2015) https://www.on-hold32.com/about/survey-results
4. Srijan Kumar, William L. Hamilton, Jure Leskovec, and Dan Jurafsky. Community Interaction and Conflict on the Web. *The Web Conference (WWW)*. 2018.
5. Falk, O., Wallinius, M., Lundström, S., Frisell, T., Anckarsäter, H., & Kerekes, N. (2014). The 1% of the population accountable for 63% of all violent crime convictions. *Social psychiatry and psychiatric epidemiology*, 49(4), 559-571. https://doi.org/10.1007/s00127-013-0783-y
6. Shojania KG, Dixon-Woods M'Bad apples': time to redefine as a type of systems problem?*BMJ Quality & Safety* 2013;22:528-531.
7. Niven, K. (2015), Can music with prosocial lyrics heal the working world? A field intervention in a call center. J Appl Soc Psychol, 45: 132-138.

PILLAR FOUR: EXPERIENCE

1. Elliot, Christopher. *These Customers Have The Best Customer Service*. Forbes. Jul 11, 2018. https://www.forbes.com/sites/christopherelliott/2018/07/11/these-companies-have-the-best-customer-service-heres-why/
2. Tsai, Wei-Chi & Huang, Yin-Mei. (2002). Mechanisms Linking Employee Affective Delivery and Customer Behavioral Intentions. The Journal of applied psychology. 87. 1001-8. 10.1037//0021-9010.87.5.1001.
3. Raport America's Top Fears, 2019. Chapman University Survey of American Fears, Retrieved from https://www.chapman.edu/wilkinson/research-centers/babbie-center/_files/americas-top-fears-2019.pdf
4. "Word Of Mouth Marketing Statistics, Fun Facts & Tips in 2020." Review42, November 21, 2020. https://review42.com/word-of-mouth-marketing-statistics/
5. 2nd, Jyoti K on January, and Miljana Mitic on April 11th. "How to Use Customer Testimonials to Generate 62% More Revenue."

The BigCommerce Blog, February

ABOUT THE AUTHOR

Michele Marshall, known as the *Queen of Customer Service*, is a Communications Trainer and Client Relations Expert. Michele has been recognized and commended for her level of customer service during her  tenure in the private sector and public sector - including Citibank, Comerica Bank, SunTrust, Sports Authority, and NYC Parks.

From 2013-2018, during her tenure as President of the Manhattan Toastmasters Club. The club achieved the status of Select and President-Distinguished Club each year. In part by creating a unique member experience.

In 2016, Michele became a Certified Professional Coach (CPC) and parlayed her training into a coaching individuals and groups to achieve their desired outcome.

In 2018, Michele Co-Founded Authentic Voice, LLC. A communication training firm designed to equip and empower individuals to become confident, polished speakers and communicators.

In 2020, she started her writing career as an Amazon Best-Selling Author with her contributions to *1 Habit for Entrepreneurial Success* and *1 Habit to Thrive in a Post-Covid*

World. Now, she embarks on solo book projects, debuting *Happy To Help.*

She enjoys exploring New York City and attending a Broadway show, when she is not working. Also, as an avid fan of films. Michele will take in the latest film releases. As well as re-watch a Star Wars, Marvel, or classic Katherine Hepburn films.

Fully embracing the philosophy of "the journey is what you make it." Michele continues to create her journey.

Visit her at marshallmichele.com

facebook.com/im2bpr31

twitter.com/im2bpr31

instagram.com/im2bpr31

linkedin.com/in/micheleannmarshall

amazon.com/author/michelemarshall

PRAISE FOR MICHELE MARSHALL

As the owner of a business that has survived recessions, powered through a pandemic, and that is currently thriving now for over 30 years. I believe that the success of any business hinges on excellent customer service. The principles and practices in this book are integral to any company's customer service team. The message and lessons are delivered in a clear, easily palpable manner.

— **JAMES CONWAY,** PRESIDENT,
JIMMY JAM PRODUCTIONS, INC.

Michele is known as the "Queen of Customer Service" for a reason. She puts her head and her heart into it. What you get is a combination of a problem solving process with a compassionate service attitude. It doesn't get much better than that in creating positive outcomes for your customers *every single time!*

— **JEANIE HOLZBACHER,**
LEADERSHIP AND HUMAN
BEHAVIOR CONSULTANT

ACKNOWLEDGMENTS

With the deepest sense of gratitude...

Unlocking the courage and audacity to take a concept to print is a challenging experience best guided by a heart-centered mentor. Someone who loves you for who you are - yet loves you too much to leave you that way. The guidance and encouragement from my mentor, **Forbes Riley**, made it possible for this book to be published. **Thank you, Forbes Riley.**

Steve Samblis, founder of 1-Habit Press, my first publisher. The one who brought my vision of being a best-selling author to life. It was a privilege to under the tutelage of an experience publisher. You made my early publishing experience so fulfilling. The bar now set very high for any future publishers.

Gloria V. Marshall. For instilling in me integrity and the value of being driven. A bit of your wisdom lives on in this book. Love you.

ALSO BY MICHELE MARSHALL

1 Habit™ for Entrepreneurial Success brought together some of the greatest Entrepreneurial Minds on the Planet and asked them each two simple questions. What is the 1 Habit that has had the most significant impact on your life? What was the 1 un-Habit you needed to get rid of to clear your pathway to success? This book is the result, and the Magic is all you need is 1 Habit to change your life Forever!

1-Habit for Entrepreneurial Success

Available Now at Amazon.com

ALSO BY MICHELE MARSHALL

After we pass through the devastation of the Covid Pandemic, the World will be a new place in many ways. To thrive in that new World will require forward-thinking and new Habits to put you back on track to a successful future. We reached out to 100 of our best-selling 1 Habit authors and asked them to envision what that World will look like and what Habits people can instill in themselves to not only survive but to thrive like never before.

This book will open your mind and heart to ways to create stability and launch your life back onto the success path you are destined for. The best part -- it all happens just 1 Habit at a time.

1-Habit to Thrive in a Post-Covid World

Available Now at Amazon.com

Get Your Team Trained Now

Your Customers deserve a
Patient, Understanding, Respectful Experience

Find out how by attending the next

Discovery Webinar

Presented by Authentic Voice, LLC

Register Today

http://authenticvoicellc.com/register

Call 917-740-0182

email info@authenticvoicellc.com

Made in the USA
Middletown, DE
08 September 2022

73505935R00108